SENSIBILITY AND CRITICISM

A Study of the Interrelation of Verbal Acts and Visual Acts

Marcus B. Hester

LANHAM • NEW YORK • LONDON

Copyright © 1983 by

University Press of America,™ Inc.

4720 Boston Way
Lanham, MD 20706

3 Henrietta Street
London WC2E 8LU England

All rights reserved
Printed in the United States of America
Library of Congress Cataloging in Publication Data

Hester, Marcus B.
   Sensibility and criticism.

   Bibliography: p.
   Includes index.
   1. Aesthetics. 2. Visual perception. I. Title.
BH39.H48   1983   111'.85   83-14580
ISBN 0-8191-3457-0 (alk. paper)
ISBN 0-8191-3458-9 (pbk. : alk. paper)

To my father,

My son, Marc,

My wife, Joan,

And the memory of my mother

ACKNOWLEDGEMENTS

I received support from several institutions and universities while working on this book. I was a fellow in the Cooperative Program in the Humanities at Chapel Hill during 1966-1967. This program was supported by the Ford Foundation. I was also supported by a Reynolds Research Leave from Wake Forest during the spring of 1975. I would like to thank these institutions and universities for their help. Persons who have especially helped me in this work on visual sensibility are many. I have learned most of what I know about visual perception from Eleanor and James Gibson, and I shall never forget their kind hospitality and helpfulness during my visit to Cornell in 1975. The person who helped me most in direct reading and criticism of the manuscript is Peter Kivy. Peter helped me, sentence by sentence, both in terms of style and philosophical substance, and I deeply appreciate his generosity with his time. My wife, Joan, suffered the inconvenience of a move to Chapel Hill for a year, and she and my son Marc missed me while I was working at Cornell. Mrs. Mary Reid, secretary of the Philosophy and German departments, cheerfully prepared version after version of this manuscript. Her humor and common sense were essential. The final version of the manuscript was typed in this exacting and perfect form by Mrs. Marie Bagby. I am grateful to these persons and institutions.

TABLE OF CONTENTS

	Page
INTRODUCTION	1
Ordinary Idioms and Definitions of Sensibility	3
Preliminary Remarks on the History of Criticism	5
Sensibility, Sensitivity and Sensing	6
Some Relevant Contemporary Analyses	7

Chapter

I	HISTORICAL ROOTS OF SENSIBILITY	13
II	SENSING	27
III	ORDINARY VISUAL ACTS	41
	Model of a Visual Act	42
IV	VISUAL ACTS AND ELEMENTS OF ART	55
	Eyeside	56
	Intermediate Aids to Direct Attention	56
	Verbal Aids to Direct Attention	63
V	ORIGINAL ELEMENTS OF ART	75
VI	SENSING AS ABILITY: STAGES AND STYLES OF SENSING	79
	First and Second Cutting Edge	80
	Styles of Sensing: Ways the Model Can Be Seated	82
	Stages of Sensing: Direction and State of Sensibility	86
VII	THE ROLES OF PAINTINGS IN DEVELOPING SENSIBILITY	95
	Models, Defining Examples and Paintings with Other Statuses	95
	Funded Experience	99

TABLE OF CONTENTS (Continued)

Chapter		Page
VIII	SOME EPISTEMOLOGICAL ISSUES	105
	Intended and Achieved Perlocutionary Force.	105
	Perlocutionary Force and Self-Knowledge.	123
	Relativism	128
IX	SENSING, ICONS AND NATURAL SIGNS.	139
	Cues and Animations Causing a Painting World: Paintings as Causally Active Fields.	140
	Sensibility as Judgment Employed on Causally Active Fields	151
	Natural Signs.	153
BIBLIOGRAPHY		161
INDEX		167

INTRODUCTION

In reading critics of painting, the viewer often has to have distinctive kinds of visual abilities in order to evaluate the critic--abilities we might characterize as various forms of sensibility. We cannot evaluate Fry's claim that Daumier's "Gar St. Lazare" is imbalanced unless we have sensibility to plastic qualities. In developing a theory of sensing or sensibility as a visual ability I use primarily two strands of argument: From certain philosophers, I develop the concept of a visual act, a kind of skilled visual ability, which can be learned. I develop a model of a visual act to show how we can learn to use our eyes, in certain ways, to look at paintings in the terms of various aesthetic positions. The other major strand of argument is my claim that critical writings about specific paintings can reasonably be construed as instructions on how to look at paintings from the critic's point of view. The critics analyzed are Reynolds, Ruskin, Baudelaire, Fry, Rosenberg and Greenberg. I claim my model of a visual act, though developed from philosophical sources, is an accurate analysis pedagogically of how we learn to look at paintings from critics. Thus I claim to have characterized the ability to sense as learned from critics. A third strand of argument, though less important, is from empirical theories of vision, especially those of J. J. Gibson. Thus, I think there is good empirical evidence for my philosophical analysis of visual ability and for my analysis of learning to see from critics, but my argument is primarily philosophical.

Just as the emphasis on sensibility as a visual ability shows what is required of the viewing subject, so it is essential to analyze the nature of the object sensed. Paintings will be understood as causally active fields which realize their impressions or cause their impressions when sensitively viewed. The entire book is limited to qualities of paintings we might classify as visual impressions. One can causally explain why one of the lines appears longer than the other in the Müller-Lyer illusion. Analogously, impressions of paintings such as balance or harmony or melancholiness can be given causal explanations. A unique peculiarity of questions about impressions of paintings is that we want to know how the painting really looks to a qualified viewer. Usually questions of how things look are related to questions of how the things really are. In the case of painting, the question is the very different one, how does the painting really look. If objects in a painting look imbalanced, they are imbalanced, while ordinarily an object may look imbalanced and not be imbalanced. In the Müller-Lyer illusion, one of the lines really looks longer than the other. Thus the book is limited to visual impressions caused by paintings in the way the Müller-Lyer illusion causes its impression. A basic thesis of my work will be that even though sensibility is a genuine visual ability, and thus is related to other forms of good visual judgment, sensibility to a painting is limited to impression of a painting--to how a painting really looks. Since sensibility to impressions is sensibility to how a painting really looks, such sensibility cannot be demonstrated in ways one shows ordinary forms of good visual judgment.

Puristic critics require us to employ purely visual abilities in sensing plastic qualities of paintings. Even before purism, critics such as Ruskin and Baudelaire often emphasized that visual ability is a necessary condition for appreciating a painting. In requiring visual sensibility alone, purists were in contrast with traditional subject matter oriented theories which emphasized taste or imagination, for example. In this book I develop a neo-purist theory of sensibility as a visual ability. My theory is neo-purist only in the sense of emphasizing visual ability, for the theory also includes naturalism and expressionism. Thus I relate the critic's and viewer's visual abilities to other purely visual skills such as those of the astronomer seeing dim galaxies or physician "reading" an x-ray. The model of a visual act I develop to explain how we learn to see and sense a painting is applicable to many other visual abilities.

We ordinarily contrast sensing as an __ability__ with occasional sensing. We may sense that someone is devious, and he may turn out to be so even though we do not usually have a good sense of character. An ability is a disposition or capacity to repeatedly do something well. Further, we often think we have sensed something when we have not sensed it. Suppose we had previously been told a certain person was devious, and had forgotten we were so told. Suppose we think we sense that he is devious. There is a good possibility that this purported sensing is not a genuine case of visually detecting (or detecting by some other sensory mode) that this person is devious. We may simply have the thought that he is devious, and since we do not remember the source of this thought we may call it "sensing." The category of occasional sensings is especially likely to be a catchall category including any lucky guesses. This qualification does not mean I do not believe there are genuine cases of occasional sensing, for I think there are perceptual cues to character, for example; and sometimes we sense these cues even though we are not generally good at perceiving that sort of thing.

Ordinary Idioms and Definitions of Sensing

Sensing as an <u>ability</u> is expressed in idioms such as having a good sense of character, a good sense of spatial composition, a good sense of depth, etc. In these cases, we are attributing to someone the ability to repeatedly detect, in some perceptual way, the quality specified. (We use these same idioms to describe abilities of painters.) I will contrast sensing as an ability or sensibility with occasional sensings. Since sensibility has no verbal form, I shall use the verb "sense" to mean an act or exercise of sensibility.

A preliminary understanding of sensing, suitable from introductory purposes, can be grasped in these definitions from <u>Webster's Third New International Dictionary</u>. Relevant definitions of the verb "sense" are:

> To perceive by the senses; to have consciousness of; feel the immanence or presence of. To become aware without express communication.

Relevant definitions of the noun "sense" are:

> A mechanism or faculty of perception--a power of interpolating or deducing from observations or unnoted stimuli in respect to a particular field or relation. Awareness or perception arrived at through or as if through interpretation of sensory stimuli; a vague and unanalyzable but persistent awareness or feeling; perception by means of the senses especially when aesthetic or emotional in content or orientation.

These definitions contain the three conditions of my

formal definition of sensibility: 1) Sensing is a perceptual act, in contrast to a cognitive act. 2) Sensing is to some perceptual subtlety, in contrast to, for example, perceptual identification of a man in normal circumstances. 3) Sensing does not involve any special background knowledge but is experientially acquired as a form of common sense.

There are many forms of sensing, of course, which are not purely aesthetic, such as having a sense of distance, direction, danger, justice or humor. I mention all these forms of sensibility, though I shall analyze only forms of sensing relevant to painting. I do not think all these ordinary forms of sensing and sensibility are entirely perceptual. A sense of justice often requires a sense of character, but it may require a feeling for legal, political and social realities as well, and these are not perceived in the direct sense that one can sense character in a caricature.

"Sense" often occurs in the idiom "gives a sense of___" as in "that painting gives a sense of cubistic space," and this particular example reminds us that we can use "give a sense of" where an illusory quality is involved. One of the lines in the Müller-Lyer illusion gives a sense of being longer than the other, and paintings usually do give a sense of space. Strictly speaking, it is only the cues which are perceived in such examples, but this tolerance of the idiom "sense of" is especially useful for covering many painting qualities. I shall argue that the ability to look at a painting sensitively is a perceptual ability, though impressions are often sensed and not perceived in a literal sense. I will analyze only passages from critics where they are dealing with impressions caused by the painting. Imbalance in a plastic sense, melancholiness in an expressionistic sense and deeper truth given by spatial and emotive qualities in a naturalistic sense are typical impressions. Besides using "sense of__" to cover impressions, "has a sense of___" or "gives a sense of___" is often also used to attribute some quality to a painting. Also "having a sense of___" is equally often used, as emphasized above, to attribute visual ability to a person.

Sensibility attributed to painters in idioms such as "has a sense of color" is a concept used to characterize a painter's excellence, in some specific way, in constructing a painting. The viewer is not of course usually capable of executing such paintings and a viewer cannot be expected to feel about paints, materials, techniques, etc., the way the painter does. However, all the critics mentioned here, and all that I know of, think the viewer has some counterpart of the faculty or ability which was involved in executing a painting, and it is this counterpart ability in the viewer by which the viewer understands the painting and by which the painting works. Reynolds, Ruskin, Baudelaire, Fry, and Rosenberg argue that the viewer has to have respectively taste, imagination, sensibility, and tactile imagination to experience a painting the way it should be experienced. My model of a visual act will show how a viewer learns the relevant visual ability from verbal functions of these critics.

Preliminary Remarks on the History of Criticism

The concept of sensibility in a purely visual sense came to be emphasized when painting ceased to be a liberal art (French Impressionism and Post-Impressionism) in the sense of interpreting religious, historical and mythological subject matter. Thus a viewer with visual sensibility is not expected to have a knowledge of literary, mythological or religious symbols. Instead, sensibility is very demanding visually.[1] Visual sensibility was used by traditional critics when they show how abstract elements of art--such as color schemes, plastic composition, light or line drawing--reinforce or are in tension with the incident of the subject matter. Sensibility was not, however, the only ability that traditional critics exercised on paintings, but for Bell and Fry and many modern critics it is the only requisite ability. Traditional paintings in fact stand up quite well to the high visual demands of a modern sensibility. These historical comments do not mean I disparage traditional art historical studies such as iconography. I view sensing as a natural complement to a study of the meaning of icons. Even Panofsky emphasizes visual sensing to show that the emotive tones, etc., of figures in paintings fit his iconographic interpretations.[2] Sensibility can, however, be employed independently of knowledge of iconography or other forms of symbolisms. Also, historically, purism was the first aesthetic position to emphasize that visual sensing was the sole and sufficient ability required of the viewer. Bell claimed that we need bring nothing to a painting but a sense of form, color and three dimensional space.[3] Since the demise of classical purism, critics of expressionistic and naturalistic types have shown that sensing can be used for their aesthetic positions also, though they often do not use verbs or idioms explicitly referring to sensing. I shall develop a theory of sensing which can include purism, expressionism and naturalism. Further, traditional critics such as Baudelaire and Ruskin anticipated the concept of visual sensing, as will be shown below.

Sensibility, Sensitivity and Sensing

I distinguish sensibility from sensitivity, but it is not as though these concepts are opposites. Sensitivity is a part of sensibility. Sensitivity means responsiveness to some one thing, quality, quantity, etc. A highly sensitive light meter is sensitive to one range of phenomenon. A sensitive person is one responsive to a narrowly specifiable object, such as being very sensitive to insults or to the status of one's birth, or sensitive to inflammatory agents like poison ivy. Some have skin sensitive to the sun. In none of these uses would "sensibility" be the correct expression. Sensibility means responsiveness to many variables and a feeling for the weighting of these variables in a given situation. Sensibility includes ability to deal with context. A person with a sense of justice has a feeling for all the variables in a moral or judicial context as well as a feeling for the weighting of relevant variables. A sense of humor may depend on a feeling for the full range of human foolishness as well as a keen perceptiveness to the full range of human nature. A tennis player with a highly developed sense of position is sensitive to a wide range of variables, with a feeling for the weighting of the variables. The variables include the speed of the ball, the position of the opponent, a feeling for his own motor abilities in terms of range, etc. A sense of position may be involved in one act--hitting the ball--but the act is made up of a rich range of variables which must be sorted out. "Sensibility" will here mean a more contextual ability than "sensitivity," but sensibility is related to sensitivity. Sensitivity to a full range of variables relevant to some act or activity, with a feeling for the weighting of these variables, is what sensibility is. Thus various sensitivities are important aspects of sensibility.

Some Relevant Contemporary Analyses

An interesting way of thinking of sensing is in terms of Dretske's analysis of "seeing that."[4] Dretske shows that seeing that presupposes a background of beliefs such that the seeing provides an increment necessary for some knowledge. One can see that the water is boiling, given some knowledge of kettles, water, etc. There are several modifications we have to make on Dretske's analysis, however, to make it appropriate to sensing. What one brings to a painting is not just beliefs, but sometimes abilities and faculties, such as taste, imagination, and sensibility. In most of Dretske's examples, not much is demanded of vision to see that something is the case, but the whole point of my theory of sensibility is that sometimes much is demanded of vision in viewing paintings. Thus it is not only background beliefs, but also visual abilities which may be required of a viewer. Traditional critics often did not place this much emphasis on vision, as just noted, but they did emphasize other faculties, such as imagination and taste. Further, the idea of an increment in Dretske's analysis sounds rather too utilitarian for a visual experience which may be worthwhile in itself. Even though traditional critics do not emphasize vision as much as do modern critics, seeing a painting has always been important. What else one is doing while viewing, as exercising taste or imagination, is also usually important in traditional critics. Modern exponents of purely visual sensibility emphasize that no other faculty or ability is necessarily exercised while viewing, but even for traditional critics, the visual experience is too important to describe as an increment for some knowledge. The purpose of viewing is not merely seeing that something is the case, but having a high quality experience of viewing. Dretske did not intend to analyze sensing paintings, and thus these remarks are not critical but expository.

Sibley in his well-known essay on aesthetic concepts argues that critics employ non-aesthetic terms and reach aesthetic conclusions, but the gap between aesthetic and non-aesthetic has to be bridged by some special faculty or ability, as, for example, taste or sensibility.[5] I agree with Schwyzer's criticism of Sibley that this is a false impression of critical practice. Critical concepts are aesthetic from the ground up.[6] Critical descriptions, characteristizations, interpretations, and explanations are already loaded with aesthetic concepts as defined by the critic, and thus the conclusion following a description is not different in kind from the description. If one accepts a critic's descriptions, characterizations, visual analyses, interpretations, etc., one is well on the way to accepting his conclusions. But even though I disagree with Sibley about the nature of descriptions, interpretations, characterizations and explanations which are the reasons for some evaluative conclusion, I agree with him that the gap between reasons and conclusions is filled by some kind of <u>judgment as an ability</u>. My theory of visual sensibility is just such an ability, and thus I attempt to give detail for how the gap between various kinds of reasons and conclusions is bridged in a purely visual manner. I do not deal with all relations of reasons and conclusions in criticism. I deal only with reasons and conclusions about impressions of paintings, and ultimately I shall give a theory showing how visual impressions are caused.

A more substantial disagreement with Sibley is that I will emphasize that sensibility is a visual ability <u>of the same species as other forms of good visual judgment</u>. Thus, unlike Sibley, I do not think there is any special faculty or ability appropriate to aesthetic qualities having to do with paintings. Taste is a faculty, but not an ability, and my theory of visual sensibility will place it distinctly among ordinary visual abilities.

Margolis argues, correctly I think, that Sibley's position is equivocal on the question of the objectivity of aesthetic judgments.[7] My analysis is intended to fill the gap Margolis says Sibley would need to fill to make his theory unequivocally objectivistic, namely a theory of perception and perceptual qualities which would justify construing aesthetic qualities as perceptual qualities.[8] I will argue in my theory of visual acts that we learn to perceive paintings in the same way that we develop any form of good perceptual judgment. In filling the gap which makes Sibley's point of view equivocal on the question of objectivism, of course, I disagree with Margolis' relativism and hold a position more like Beardsley's.[9] I will claim, as does Beardsley, that many aesthetic judgments are true. I will even claim that they are more than true, a concept I shall call "truth-plus." Successful critical judgments are more than true in the sense that they express unexpressed sensings, highlight facts we had not noted before and characterize in a way we had not thought of before, thus structuring and restructuring what I shall call funded experience.

Another analysis that is fruitful in adumbrating my position is in Peter Kivy's Speaking of Art. Kivy argues that there are three ways aesthetic concepts could be condition governed:

> The strong way in which "prime number" is condition-governed; 2) the looser way in which "intelligent" is condition-governed; and 3) the altogether different way in which "red" is condition-governed in virtue of there being normal conditions of perception and perceiver.[10]

Kivy, in criticizing Sibley, argues convincingly that aesthetic concepts are condition-governed in the second sense. My emphasis on sensibility as a perceptual ability falls under Kivy's third kind of condition-governed concept. Kivy himself points out that the necessity for some sort of perceptual ability for the correct application of aesthetic concepts is by no means inconsistent with his own view that such concepts are condition-governed in the second sense. Perceptual abilities, which Gombrich calls "the prognostic purpose of perception,"[11] allow talented perceivers to do quickly and efficiently what we can all do by mundane techniques, and the possibility of specifying the mundane procedures shows how these concepts can be condition-governed.

The thrust of these remarks is to suggest that the whole idea of the logic of criticism is misleading when interpreted as a study in relations between remarks about impressions of specific works and conclusions about those impressions of specific works. If one does bother to isolate out a critic's reasons from his conclusions, one will have a rather unrewarding exercise in finding logical fallacies. The real force of a critic's conclusions about impressions of specific paintings derives not from logic, but from judgment as an ability, an ability specified in the critic's aesthetic where he specified what faculties, abilities, knowledge and experience constitute an ideal viewer. Of course, a critic does argue for the basic terms of his criticism, argue for the role art should play in life, argue for the application of his terms to a certain painter, etc. These arguments can be evaluated logically. But the force of reasons about impressions of specific works to conclusions about impressions of specific works cannot be logically evaluated. The critic often gives such scant reasons for his conclusions because he assumes the real force of his reasons will be derived from the viewer's judgment. But the descriptions, characterizations, explanations and interpretations which may serve for reasons for various kinds of conclusions must be clear enough to direct the viewer's visual attention, and thus his sensibility as trained judgment, to the relevant part or way of looking at the painting. I emphasize that I will deal only with critical reasons and conclusions about impressions caused by paintings. Critics give other sorts of arguments (reasons and conclusions) which do not involve sensibility as a visual ability.

If the real connection between a critic's reasons and conclusions about impressions of paintings is in abilities, then the reasons do not function like reasons in a logical argument. The critic's reasons function in either of two ways: 1) One can use the reasons (expressed in characterizations, descriptions, explanations and interpretations) to redirect one's attention so that one employs the relevant faculties and abilities one already has; or, 2) one can use the reasons (expressed in the characterizations, descriptions, etc.) as terms from which one can learn a relevant mode of attention. If one cannot see the details of a dim galaxy, one has to either redirect one's attention, assuming one is skilled in averted vision, or one has to learn the relevant way of attending. Sibley correctly saw that "reasons" in criticism are really directors of attention.

The rational of my chapter order is this: Initially, sensing as a visual ability can be understood as a visual skill. Like any skill, it can be learned analytically by isolating and practicing the various aspects of the skill. In Chapter III, analytical detail is given with regard to ordinary visual acts, and in Chapter IV, this detail is extended to analytically learning to sense from critics. Learning to sense in certain terms initially seems to pose a problem with original elements of art. The very concept of skill suggests fixity to a specialized context, and in Chapter V the emphasis on sensing as a visual skill is softened. It is there argued that sensing in certain terms is not stultifying to original elements of art. Analytical learning to see can be assimilated by our perceptual-motor mechanism, our eye-mind, in an indefinite number of levels and styles of sensing, and these are characterized in Chapter VI. In Chapter VIII, I discuss the way stages and styles of sensing affect and make possible certain epistemological successes and failures of passages from criticism. A passage is successful if we find it incisive, sound, witty, perceptive, etc. A passage from a critic fails if we find it academic, insensitive, distorting, based on a misunderstanding of the painter, etc. In Chapter IX, a theory of natural symbolism is developed to make full sense of the special kind of knowledge which is a constitutive part of sensing.

ENDNOTES

[1] I analyze the nature of sensibility through the model of visual acts developed below.

[2] Erwin Panofsky, Studies in Iconology: Humanistic Themes in the Art of the Renaissance (New York, Evanston and London: Harper Torchbooks, 1962), pp. 3-17.

[3] Clive Bell, Art (New York: Capricorn Books, 1958), p. 28.

[4] Fred J. Dretske, Seeing and Knowing (Chicago: The University of Chicago Press, 1969), esp. pp. 78-139.

[5] Frank Sibley, "Aesthetic Concepts," The Philosophical Review, 68 (October, 1959), pp. 421-50.

[6] H. R. G. Schwyzer, "Sibley's 'Aesthetic Concepts'," The Philosophical Review, 72 (January, 1963), pp. 72-78.

[7] Joseph Margolis, ed., Philosophy Looks at the Arts: Contemporary Readings in Aesthetics, Revised ed. (Philadelphia: Temple University Press, 1978), p. 392.

[8] Ibid., p. 391.

[9] Ibid., p. 383.

[10] Peter Kivy, Speaking of Art (The Hague: Martinus Nijhoff, 1973), p. 5.

[11] R. L. Gregory and E. H. Gombrich, eds., Illusion in Nature and Art (New York: Charles Scribner's Sons, 1973), p. 218.

CHAPTER I

HISTORICAL ROOTS OF SENSIBILITY

One helpful way of thinking about the more abstract theorizing a critic does--in contrast to his descriptions, interpretations, explanations and characterizations of specific paintings--is as a specification of some disjunct of faculties, abilities, knowledge or experience expected of an ideal viewer. The critic usually develops this specification in justifying the basic terms of his criticism. Statements about what makes great art are usually explicitly connected to claims about the abilities, faculties, knowledge and experience the critic thinks necessary to fully understand and appreciate his models or paradigms of excellence. This connection means that statements about what makes great art summarize the direction an amateur viewer would need to take in order to fully understand and appreciate the stated paradigms of excellence. These paradigms of excellence, plus statements about how they are to be viewed, define the ultimate in aesthetic experience for that critic. It will be helpful to give a quick sketch of what critics have expected of ideal viewers in order to show the historical roots, in criticism of painting, of my theory of sensing.

Reynolds thought great art had ideal beauty and grand style, and he tells us how we achieve knowledge and taste to know both. By studying the forms of nature one can sense their deformity and thus get an intimation of the ideal.

> The most beautiful forms have something
> about them like weakness, minuteness, or
> imperfection. But it is not every eye
> that perceives these blemishes. It must
> be an eye long used to the contemplation
> and comparison of these forms; and which,
> by long habit of observing what any set of
> objects of the same kind have in common,
> has acquired the power of discerning what
> each wants in particular.[1]

Both the painter and viewer need this study of the blemishes of natural forms in order to sense ideal beauty. Understanding great style has related requirements. Grand style is the

>art of animating and dignifying the figure
>with intellectual grandeur, of impressing
>the appearance of philosophic wisdom, or
>heroic virtue. This can only be acquired
>by him that enlarges the sphere of his
>understanding by a variety of knowledge,
>and warms his imagination with the best
>productions of ancient and modern poetry.[2]

Baudelaire was in many ways a traditional critic, for he thought Delacroix, the last great traditional painter, was the most original painter of all times. Thus Baudelaire employs an imagination warmed "with the best productions of ancient and modern poetry." But Baudelaire's theory of the imagination is also forward looking to a modern theory of sensibility, for the imagination is a <u>perceptive</u> faculty. Imagination perceives the emotive tone of the elements used in painting. For example, it perceives that "yellow, orange and red inspire and express the ideas of joy, richness, glory and love."[3] The imagination is the queen of the faculties, and it perceives "the moral meaning of colour, of contour, of sound and scents."[4] Under the influence of Poe, Baudelaire attributes to the imagination the power to sense ideational and transcendent meanings of color. Even without recourse to opium, we sometimes experience perceptive states

>when the senses are keener and sensations
>more ringing, when the firmament of a more
>transparent blue plunges headlong into an
>abyss more infinite, when sounds chime like
>music, when colours speak, and scents tell
>of whole worlds of ideas.[5]

The imagination senses cross-sensory analogies, and these are the basis of the unity of the arts. In summary the imagination, then, perceives the emotive tone of color, its ideational and transcendent aspects, its cross-sensory analogies and metaphors and its moral meaning. Baudelaire does not seem to believe color has this sort of meaning by <u>association</u> with significant events. Rather, his understanding of the perceptive powers of the imagination is more in line with the theories of gestalt psychologists and phenomenologists who hold that parts and wholes in our experience intrinsically have meaning. Baudelaire thus anticipates a modern theory of sensing in that he thinks other elements of art, in addition to subject matter, have intrinsic meaning. I will similarly relate sensing to a theory of natural signs (Chapter IX).

Ruskin also emphasizes that the imagination is a perceptive faculty which is related to truth or insight into nature. Like Baudelaire, he clearly states that we can sense the meaning of certain forms and lines:

> A great composition always has a leading emotional purpose, technically called its motive, to which all its lines and forms have some relation. Undulating lines, for instance, are expressive of action; and would be false in effect if the motive of the picture was one of repose. Horizontal and angular lines are expressive of rest and strength; and would destroy a design whose purpose was to express disquiet and feebleness.[6]

The painter and critic then have to sense the meaning of lines, for example, in order to paint or interpret, respectively, "the soul of a scene." This sort of heteronomous point of view, which emphasizes the reinforcement of the meaning of subject matter by the meaning of the abstract elements of painting, anticipates a modern theory of sensing.[7]

In Fry, we see the importance of subject matter dropped, and Fry specifically attacks the importance of symbolism and ideas associated with subject matter. Fry as a critic could no longer presuppose a viewer whose imagination was warmed by the best products of ancient and modern poetry. In fact, Europe was increasingly flooded with art works completely detached from their culture, such as Negro sculpture, and thus the critic had to respond solely on the basis of his sensibility.

> We may suppose him (a pagan viewer of Raphael's "Transfiguration") to be moved by the pure contemplation of the spatial relations of plastic volumes. It is when we have got to this point that we seem to have isolated this extremely elusive aesthetic quality which is the one constant quality of all works of art, and which seems to be independent of all the prepossessions and associations which the spectator brings with him from his past life.[8]

Fry even speculates, in a manner consistent with my theory of natural signs in Chapter IX, on the origin of cross-cultural sensibility.

> Now it will be noticed that nearly all these emotional elements of design are connected with essential conditions of our physical existence: rhythm appeals to all the sensations which accompany muscular activity; mass to all the infinite adaptations to the force of gravity which we are forced to make; the spatial judgment is equally profound and universal in its application to life; our feeling about inclined planes is connected with our necessary judgments about the conformation of the earth itself; light again, is so necessary a condition of our existence that we become intensely sensitive to changes in its intensity. . . . It will be seen, then, that the graphic arts arouse emotions in us by playing upon what one may call the overtones of some of our primary physical needs.[9]

Hume gives a similar explanation of principles of painting. "When a building seems clumsy and tottering to the eye, it is ugly and disagreeable; tho' we be fully assur'd of the solidity of the workmanship. 'Tis a kind of fear, which causes this sentiment of disapprobation; but the passion is not the same with that which we really feel, when oblig'd to stand under a wall, that we really think tottering and insecure."[10] Fry, like Ruskin and Baudelaire, develops the idea of imagination as a perceptive faculty, but Fry's concept of the imagination makes it even more distinctly a percept al ability. The imaginative life

> must in the first place be adapted to that disinterested intensity of contemplation, which we have found to be the effect of cutting off the responsive action. It must be suited to that heightened power of perception which we found to result therefrom.[11]

> The imaginative life is distinguished by the greater clearness of its perception, and the greater purity and freedom of its emotion.[12]

16

In my theory of sensibility, I will follow Fry in emphasizing the "heightened power of perception" and "greater clearness of its perception" characteristic of visual sensibility, but I do not follow his emphasis on disinterestedness, for I feel that the latter concept has been damaged by criticisms of the aesthetic attitude.[13]

Fry explicitly identifies this perceptual ability with sensibility, and he thinks that the subconscious working through sensibility provides the cross-cultural basis on which we can ask for reasons for increasingly smaller plastic manipulations by the painter. He frankly admits that he knows many artists whose work he has discussed would be surprised at his emphasis on plastic qualities; but an advantage of the subconscious or unconscious self (Fry does not seem to distinguish these two) is that it is universal, allowing one to deal with works from radically different cultures, and, of course, the artist may well not have thought about such matters when making the work. I consider my theory of sensing and sensibility as an expansion of Fry's, making his theory suitable to include naturalism and expressionism as well as purism. Fry's theory of sensibility shows a clear change over the ability, faculty, knowledge and experience Reynolds expected of an ideal viewer. Thus Fry emphasizes sensibility as the sole ability required of a viewer. In this emphasis he goes beyond Ruskin and Baudelaire in that for them the perceptive imagination was used to sense and supplement the meaning of subject matter.

Rosenberg, the well-known contemporary interpreter of Action Painting, discusses subject matter, but the subject matter now is the artist's psychic state or tension as expressed in brush gesture.

> If the ultimate subject matter of all art is the artist's psychic state or tension (and this may be the case even in nonindividualistic epocs), that state (e.g., grief) may be represented through an abstract sign. The innovation of Action Painting was to dispense with the representation of the state in favor of enacting it in the physical movement of painting. The action on the canvas became its own representation.[14]

Action Paintings, without any recognizable subject matter, can even express landscape. The act of painting subconsciously excites the landscapes a painter has seen, and these landscapes enter his gestures.

> Long Island or Woodstock underbrush enters an abstraction by Pollock or Guston in a state too primitive for definition except as substance in general. Similarly, the relation between the gardens and sunlit walls of Provincetown and the paintings of Hans Hofmann must be established entirely by tactile imagination; the last thing one may expect to find is resemblance to detail. Here again nature begins in the artist.[15]

This last statement is reminiscent of Baudelaire's approving quote from Delacroix that "nature is nothing but a dictionary" and reminiscent of Baudelaire's statement that the artist represents his own nature.[16] Rosenberg also is explicit about the correct terms for viewing Action Painting:

> Criticism must begin by recognizing in the painting the assumptions inherent in its mode of creation. Since the painter has become an actor, the spectator has to think in a vocabulary of action: its inception, duration, direction--psychic state, concentration and relaxation of the will, passivity, alert waiting. He must become a connoisseur of the gradations between the automatic, the spontaneous, the evoked.[17]

These terms of viewing are quite different from those Reynolds recommended as an imagination warmed "with the best productions of ancient and modern poetry." The theory of sensing being developed here will be applicable to the lines, forms and colors of things in picture space, as in Baudelaire and Ruskin, as well as to the gestures in paint emphasized by Rosenberg. Thus the theory being developed here will be applicable to both representational and abstract works. Picture space can have things in it and be a place to gesture in, and we can learn to sense in terms appropriate to both.

In summary, it is obvious that for Reynolds the ideal viewer should have the faculty of taste and a knowledge of ideal beauty derived from classical works and developed by a knowledge of ancient poetry. The viewer, like the painter, must have a taste educated on the classics of Greek art and literature. The viewer is expected to have a knowledge of the liberal arts. For Ruskin, the ideal viewer should have the faculty of imagination, and imagination is explicitly contrasted with fancy and taste. One has also to have a knowledge of the details of nature, a knowledge of the underlying essence of objects and scenes in nature, and knowledge of the correct view of Nature. (Ruskin's own view of Nature changes from puritanical to romantic to a tragic sort of humanism.) One also has to be able to sense the meaning of abstract elements of art such as forms or lines. For Baudelaire, the ideal viewer is also expected to have imagination, but even though Ruskin and Baudelaire are romantics, "imagination" has a very different meaning for them. For Baudelaire, external nature is nothing but a dictionary for a great painter. The great painter follows his own nature, and here Baudelaire centers his concept more on the concept of creative genius than on a romantic concept of nature. Further, for Baudelaire the imagination is a faculty that understands cross-sensory analogies and meanings of simple elements such as color. His theory of the imagination makes imagination the queen of the faculties, and it is the source of the rich suggestiveness and allusiveness which was emphasized in the symbolic poets. Clearly Baudelaire expected his readers to have a knowledge of classical and mythological subjects, as indicated in his interpretations of works such as Delacroix's "Dante and Vergil in Hell." Painting is still a liberal art in the sense of interpreting religious, mythological and historical subjects. In Fry, we definitely see painting ceasing to be a liberal art in this sense, despite his defense of it as a liberal art in the beginning of <u>Last Lectures</u>. Instead, sensibility as a visual ability is the main requirement of an ideal viewer. Works torn from their historical and cultural contexts can still be appreciated by sensibility, as in Fry's high ranking of Negro sculpture. The development of a concept of sensibility made appreciation possible in a context where one was inundated with works from foreign and often primitive cultures. Sensibility was, in a sense, the lowest common denominator, a feeling we share with the Negro artist about whose culture we know nothing. Appreciating paintings no longer requires a knowledge of mythological and classical sources. Rosenberg suggests that tactile imagination is the way landscapes become embodied in Action Paintings, and the viewer and critic must become conoisseurs "of the gradations between the automatic, the spontaneous, the evoked."[18]

The change in the history of painting to sensing, as I shall define it, was not of the nature of still another aesthetic position. Rather, it was like a new way of experiencing paintings which cuts across or includes a range of aesthetic positions. The historical shift to an emphasis on sensing was more like the radical change in the late Middle Ages from a purposive system of explanation to a mechanical one. I think there were three basic factors contributing to this change which took place in the history of painting, so far as I can tell, around 1860. First, painting ceased to be a liberal art in the sense of interpreting religious, historical, and mythological subjects. The painter could no longer expect the viewer to be familiar with such matters because the influence of technological life had so eaten away at their importance. The question became: Given some severe limits on the nature of the knowledge the viewer might be expected to have, what is left of the possibilities for painting? Forms of purism, expressionism, and naturalism have attempted to survive these basic changes, and my analysis of sensibility is based on the belief that we can learn to see under these new conditions.[19] Traditional painters practiced some of the elements of art that can be sensed, but not these elements of art exclusively. Second, because of photography, painting no longer had the assured role of recording identifiable and recognizable objects. In place of these functions, the question became: What can the visual image alone, to the trained eye, do and mean visually? Third, the presence of large numbers of foreign works, without knowledge of their culture, required some purely visual basis for appreciation. As Fry speculates, perhaps all we have in common with some unknown Negro Artist, for example, is a feeling for plastic qualities developed in ordinary motor activities.

More comments are needed on the relation of sensibility to romanticism. Generally, I think there were two strands in the meaning of the concept of sensibility, and both strands can still be seen in lexical entries. There was a romantic strand in which sensibility was an extreme emotional responsiveness, a hypersensitivity, a sensitivity that is a susceptibility, a sensitivity suggesting extreme delicacy and frailty before life's emotions. This kind of sensibility was often connected with melancholia and similar states, and can be seen in some of Jane Austin's characters in Sense and Sensibility. Baudelaire's concept of the imagination, with his emphasis upon the romanticism and melancholiness of the genius of art, is related to this strand of the concept (and to the other as well). This is not the strand of the concept I am interested in.

Another strand emphasized sensibility as a refined perception. Hume's concept of taste is in this tradition:

> Where the organs are so fine, as to allow nothing to escape them; and at the same time so exact as to perceive every ingredient in the composition: This we call delicacy of taste. . . .[20]

Also Hume thinks, as I shall argue below, that this sort of refined perception can be improved by practice.

> But allow him to acquire experience in those objects, his feeling becomes more exact and nice. He not only perceives the beauties and defects of each part, but marks the distinguishing species of each quality, and assigns it suitable praise or blame. . . . The mist dissipates, which seemed formerly to hang over the object: The organ acquires greater perfection in its operations; and can pronounce, without danger of mistake, concerning the merits of every performance. In a word, the same address and dexterity, which practice gives the execution of any work, is also acquired by the same means, in the judging of it.[21]

Hume here correctly avoids the belief in the innocent or untrained eye. Other critics in this second strand of the concept of sensibility, the strand emphasizing sensibility as a perceptual ability, have shared with the romantic strand the belief in the innocent eye. My theory is distinctly in Hume's tradition as the emphasis on learning to sense will make obvious.

All the critics mentioned, except Reynolds, emphasize that perceptual ability is at least an aspect of understanding paintings. Baudelaire's concept of correspondence and his later concept of the imagination emphasized a kind of perception which can discern cross-sensory analogies, the deeper meaning of color, and whole realms of ideas aroused by color (and other elements). He compares imagination to a kind of perception which is so keen as to be hallucinative. Ruskin also attributes perceptual powers to the imagination. One of the main functions of the imagination was called penetrative imagination, that ability by which the artist sensed the soul of a scene, and Ruskin in his concept of truth argues for refined perception as necessary to sense truth. And, of course, Fry understands sensibility as a form of perception.[22] As to Rosenberg, his concept of the nature of artistic production is closer to mine, as examined elsewhere,[23] than to any of the other critics, except that I emphasize experience with elements of art instead of the subconscious operating in acts of painting. Rosenberg also in places contrasts the rational with the subconscious, and places the highest value on the subconscious. I reject this version of romanticism. My concept of sensibility, in summary, is definitely in the second strand of the concept, and I shall mean by it a kind of refined perception, a distinctly perceptual act of sensing which is to be formally defined in the next chapter.

Romantic theories of sensibility divorce it from rational faculties and methods. My theory, on the contrary, makes it redundant with rational faculties, but redundant in this special sense: Most forms of sensibility are exercised in a context with a time dimension, such that one has to make a decision on the basis of elusive perceptual cues <u>before</u> other rational evidence or procedures are available. Sometimes something would never be discovered unless one made a leap of faith based on what one sensed. James seems to have thought that we sometimes have to act on the basis of intuition to find out what other people are like or what they think of us.[24] Often, after the fact, the perceptual judgment turns out to be a good one, as shown by redundant sources of information. In fact, having sensibilities of various forms simply means that one frequently makes good judgments on the basis of the elusive cues. Gombrich described this sort of perception as having a prognostic character.[25] In sports, many decisions have to be made without deliberation; and if one can consistently make such decisions in the right way, one is said to have a good sense of distance, a good sense of court position, etc. Someone with a good sense of character knows how to key in on subtle perceptual cues as to what a person is like, and later decisions and actions of the person judged must confirm the judgment for us to say that the judge has a good sense of character. There will be some peculiarities of judgment in aesthetic contexts which remove the possibility in any direct sense of these sorts of success-testing of various forms of sensibility. Here I merely indicate that I do not consider my theory of sensibility a romantic theory in the sense of divorcing the sort of perceptual intuition that is sensibility from rational faculties involving matters such as inference and calculation.

ENDNOTES

[1] Sir Joshua Reynolds, Discourses on Art, ed. Robert R. Wark (San Marino, Calif." Huntington Library, 1959), p. 44.

[2] Ibid., p. 50.

[3] Charles Baudelaire, Art in Paris, 1845-1862: Salons and Other Exhibitions, trans. and ed. by Jonathan Mayne (London: Phaidon Press, 1965), p. 160.

[4] Ibid., p. 156.

[5] Ibid., p. 143.

[6] John Ruskin, Modern Painters (London: George Allen, 1903), V, 164.

[7] See Beardsley for an explanation of "heteronomous." Monroe C. Beardsley, Aesthetics: Problems in the Philosophy of Criticism (New York, Chicago, San Francisco, Atlanta: Harcourt, Brace and World, 1958), pp. 293-302.

[8] Roger Fry, Vision and Design (New York: Meridian Books, 1960), pp. 298-99.

[9] Ibid., pp. 34-35.

[10] David Hume, A Treatise of Human Nature, ed. L. A. Selby-Bigge (Oxford, The Clarendon Press, 1958), p. 586.

[11] Fry, p. 29.

[12] Ibid., p. 24.

[13] See George Dickie, Art and the Aesthetic: An Institutional Analysis (Ithaca and London: Cornell University Press, 1974), pp. 53-134.

[14] Harold Rosenberg, The Anxious Object: Art Today and Its Audience (New York and Toronto: Mentor, 1969), p. 125.

[15] Ibid., p. 69. This remark is reminiscent of Baudelaire's claim that the artist's purpose is to realize his own nature.

[16] Baudelaire, pp. 155, 159.

[17] Harold Rosenberg, The Tradition of the New (New York and Toronto: McGraw-Hill, 1965), p. 29.

[18] Ibid., p. 29.

[19] I consider the experiments in painting, beginning with French Impressionism, to be perhaps the only future for painting, and I share some of Kandinsky's dreams about the possibilities of purely visual, and even abstract, elements of art having as rich a range of possibilities as music. See Wassily Kandinsky, Concerning the Spiritual in Art, and Painting in Particular, trans. Michael Sadleir, Francis Golffing, Michael Harrison and Ferdinand Ostertag (New York, George Wittenborn, 1966), p. 40. See pp. 43-67 for details on color and form as an abstract language.

[20] David Hume, Of the Standard of Taste and Other Essays, ed., John W. Lenz (Indianapolis, New York, Kansas City: Bobbs-Merrill, 1965), p. 11.

[21] Ibid., p. 13.

[22] But with Fry, it is important to make my disagreements clear. Both Bell and Fry in places assume that the aesthetic attitude is a unique emotion, perhaps being influenced in this view by G. E. Moore. At other places they make some simple positivistic assumptions about seeing. Fry also accepts Tolstoy's formulation of questions about art and the emotions, though Fry gives the opposite answer. Contrary to these views, I think we have to learn to sense a painting, and sensibility to a painting has continuity with ordinary forms of sensibility. In saying ordinary experience provides a background of visual normalcy which is exploited in elements of art, I will not mean that one does not have to learn to employ this background and learn for what ends it has been exploited. Some of this learning is through activities in our form of life, and some from the language of critics, and the two are ultimately a unity. There is a good deal of the "innocent eye" theory in both Bell and Fry, and I think my model makes clear that I do not believe in the innocent eye.

[23] Marcus Hester, "Purpose in Painting and Action," *American Philosophical Quarterly*, 7, No. 1 (January, 1970), pp. 62-73.

[24] William James, *The Will to Believe and Other Essays in Popular Philosophy* (New York: Longmans, Green and Co., 1897), pp. 2-25. Reprinted in Amelie Rorty, ed., *Pragmatic Philosophy: An Anthology* (Garden City, N. Y.: Anchor Books, 1966), pp. 191-94.

[25] Gregory and Gombrich, p. 218.

CHAPTER II

SENSING

For clarity, it seems best first to give a formal definition of sensing and then defend the definition in the analysis of examples from critics. The defense of the stipulations will require the entire book. Further, I claim this definition of sensing is consistent with the ordinary definitions already given. I do formalize sensing into a theory below. I shortly give necessary and jointly sufficient conditions for sensing impressions of paintings, but first some comments are necessary on the concepts of impressions and cues.

I use "sensing impressions of paintings" mainly out of grammatical convenience, the phrase being short for "sensing how a painting appears or looks." "Sensing an appearance of a painting" or "sensing the look of a painting" are awkard and ungrammatical. What I mean to cover by "impressions" then includes the actual physical qualities of a painting, but, more importantly, the qualities caused by the painting, such as picture space. A painting causes impressions by exploiting cues from ordinary perception. An ordinary cue to space, texture, for example, can be used so a painting will give a sense of space. I use the concept "cue" inclusively, to cover diverse ways impressions of paintings are caused. These vary from strictly physiological causes to indirect effects which presuppose types of experience and knowledge. Also I will use the concept of cues to cover similarities in the painting image to ordinary objects, similarities which vary from the merest hint or suggestion to full realism. These cues cause the painting image to be animated by the qualities and tones of the ordinary object. In short, given the nature of the eye and how it is deeply conditioned by experience, the painter can exploit a wide range of cues to give a wide range of impressions. What I am calling "impressions of paintings" are caused in the same sense as the Müller-Lyer illusion.[1]

With these preliminaries aside, I give these necessary and jointly sufficient conditions for sensing impressions of paintings. The main numbered conditions are conditions defining any form of sensing. The more stringent subconditions, separately listed as 1', etc., are defining conditions of sensing impressions of paintings.

1) The Perceptual Condition. Sensing is not a mode of cognition, but a mode of visual perception. If one infers something from a painting, one does not sense that something in the painting. Further, if one remembers something one has read about a painting, and remembers only, one is not sensing, since sensing is a mode of perception. Sensing, being perceptual, is immediate and not inferential.[2] "Sense" is inappropriate in describing a cognitive act such as inference, since sensing is a preceptual mode.

Perception is, of course, a very complex concept, and it has many conditions of its own. The special kind of visual judgment I am calling sensing has all these same conditions, plus the additional ones analyzed shortly. There is not space here, nor is my interest here, to develop a general theory of perception. It is sufficient to simply state that I accept Chisholm's analysis of perception, with qualifications not relevant here, in the Second Edition of Theory of Knowledge.[3]

Since sensing is a mode of perception, one can sense something only when there is something to sense, and thus "sense" is a success verb. One might argue that "sense" is not a success word because it is used to make a weaker epistemological claim than "see." A common retort to a rumor that someone is devious might go "you do not really know he is devious, you only sense that he is." But even though it is true that "sense" is weaker epistemologically than "see," and thus is weaker evidence, not being admissible in court for example, it is still a success word. If the purportedly devious person is later clearly shown not to be devious, even the weaker epistemological claim to have sensed that he was devious has to be taken back.

Sensing is a mode of vision in the sense of a visual act of discounting and emphasizing. I will emphasize below that we have considerable ability to learn how to look at things, and my model of a visual act will emphasize ways we can deliberately learn to sense something. I will compare sensing to other modes of skilled perception such as averted vision in astronomy. The eyes themselves can be used in different modes of looking at something, as in visual focusing, blurring or scanning. Devices can be placed between the eye and object to enhance and deemphasize. The object itself can be changed so as to make what is looked for more obvious. In a literal sense, these are acts of perception, and they can be learned as any skill.

1') But an important qualification is necessary on the Perceptual Condition since I am defining sensing of impressions. Only the cues of some impression are really seen. If we claim something gives a sense of danger, we are claiming there are real cues to danger even if we cannot specify them. The cues may be only potentially specifiable, for even in such well-known illusion illustrations as the Müller-Lyer illusion, the cues which make one of the lines seem longer than the other are not now specifiable. But if sensing is a mode of perception, there must be cues causing the impression. The reason we do not say the impression is perceived, but only sensed, is that impressions, especially illusionistic ones, are about objects not really there to be perceived. We do not really see space in a painting, but we do sense it, and we must see the cues causing the impression. I am defining sensing so that it is distinguishable from imagining something a certain way, and the way I shall draw the distinction is to give, as already begun, a causal analysis of impressions such that the cues to impressions caused by paintings must be actually visual. Sensing a painting's impressions is not just something done while perceiving, as one might imagine a painting a certain way while perceiving. The painting must visually cause the impression for sensing to be a genuine perceptual act. There is something we see in the Müller-Lyer illusion which causes one of the lines to appear longer than the other. The impressions of paintings are caused in the same way.

There seems to be a contradiction involved in my claims: All instances of visual sensing are instances of perception (perception is a necessary condition of sensing). Some instances of sensing, most of those discussed in this book, in fact, involve illusionistic qualities. No instances of sensing illusionistic qualities are instances of perception. Thus some instances of sensing both are and are not modes of perception. As noted, to say that sensing must take place during perception is not strong enough. We may imagine, dream or fantasize while perceiving a painting, as we all know. In contrast, sensing is a genuine perceptual act. The impression sensed must be caused, in some direct sense of "caused," by visual cues in the painting, and these cues are perceived.[4] Still, some qualification is needed to make the concept of perceptual illusion not contradictory. The best way out of this contradiction is to deny the last premise--to deny that no instances of sensing illusionistic qualities are instances of perception. Some distinctions will be helpful: The act of sensing is a genuine perceptual act. Throughout this book it is treated as a form of perceptual act, and it is refined the way other perceptual acts are refined. The trouble is with the object sensed. Only the visual cues are seen, the impression being caused. The act of sensing is genuinely a perceptual act. In the same way, sensing the Müller-Lyer illusion has a queer status. Seeing the illusion is a genuine case of seeing, and we do not just project or dream or fantasize the illusion into existence. But it is only the cues which are literally seen, the impression being caused in a direct sense. Throughout this book, the Perceptual Condition will mean sensing is a perceptual act in this somewhat stretched sense. We do speak of perceptual illusions, and they are distinctly different from other forms of illusion and delusion.

Critics who are analytically minded often specify cues which are purportedly causing a specified impression. These cues are important in analytically learning how to sense the qualities of paintings. If one attends to the cues in the proper terms and units of attention, the impression will be more obvious. Sibley in his essay "Aesthetic Concepts" gives many examples where some impression is explained by a well-known correlation, such as that low keyed colors tend to cause delicacy.[5] Of course, one can learn to sense in terms of the qualities without specifying the cues, and this synoptic form of sensing is just as important as more analytical attention. My model of a visual act will show how both kinds of sensing can be learned. By emphasizing the necessity of visual cues in the definition of sensing impressions, I am excluding from the definition non-perceptual ways of knowing something such as danger (for example, inference). Also sensing an impression of a painting is not imagining or fantasizing an impression while seeing a painting. The painting must directly cause the impression.

2) The Subtlety Condition. Sensing is an elusive way of perceptually grasping something, as sensing danger where we cannot say exactly how we are per-

ceiving it. In ordinary usage, two meanings of this elusive perception are conflated: One may perceive something by a sense that is not definite, something like a sixth sense; or one may perceive cues one cannot specify. The latter will be emphasized here; and, given the Perceptual Condition above, I emphasize that if one is genuinely sensing <u>perceptually</u>, the cues by which one is sensing are potentially specifiable. Perceptual sensing is the refined use of an ordinary perceptual mode, not a sixth sense.

The Subtlety Condition defines sensing as a subclass of visual perception. More specifically, sensing is <u>not</u> obvious recognition of a particular or identification of a type. Sensing always involves more subtle cues than those noticed in recognizing a particular or identifying a type. One does not sense a man in Holbein's "Erasmus of Rotterdam." Of course, the fact that one is sensing some impression in a painting does not mean one <u>fails</u> to recognize a particular or identify a type. As Ziff points out, without identifying types, one might well misperceive some aesthetic quality.[6] Put differently, one sees a man in Holbein's "Erasmus." No subtle perception is involved in identifying a man, though one does sense Erasmus' nature.

The concept of cues, in the expanded sense used here, is also relevant to the Sublety Condition. A cue is by definition something elusive. Anything obviously seen or obviously connected to something else is not a cue to anything. As Austin remarked in a very different context, if I see a loaf of bread in the bread box, in good light, etc., there are not just clues that there is bread there.[7] Analogously, a cue is a subtle sign, and thus an act of sensing, given the Subtlety Condition, must involve cues. Of course, as already suggested, many things seen or identified or recognized may have indirect relevance to sensing, for sensing might fail unless we identify the obvious. But we do not call a visual act sensing unless elusive cues are involved. Sensing is a highly skilled form of perception.

Sensing is often involved in <u>non-aesthetic</u> forms of recognition or identification. <u>No doubt</u> Friedlander has considerable ability to sense forgeries. An X-ray technician or physician learns to sense disorders from X-rays. But even here these non-aesthetic forms of sensing imply a subtle perceptual act. Friedlander does not sense that there is a painting before him, nor the technician that these very familiar negatives are X-ray photographs. There are a number of things we obviously see about any painting, but we do not speak of sensing these things.

2') A helpful way of thinking of sensing impressions of painting, as well as other forms of good visual judgment, is in terms of sensibility to multiple variables in a rich context. Thus, sensing involves more of a feeling for context than sensitivity. Sensing is of subtleties of cues and counter cues. For example, Fry claims Daumier's "Gar St. Lazare" is imbalanced. There are multiple variables which can create imbalance (or balance):[8] The positions of the figures (the actual one Fry claims), the masses of the figures due to visual textures, the sizes of the figures, the role colors might play in composition, etc. Fry does not mention all these; but, from other examples concerning balance, it is clear that these sorts of considerations are relevant to balance. Again, Fry does not give the variables a definite weighting, but if one countered Fry by saying that the visual texture of the main figure gave it a certain massiveness which overcame the problems of placement, Fry might well say in this instance--and perhaps generally--that placement was the overriding variable. To know whether in fact the placement of the figure in this painting gives a sense of imbalance, to know how to sort out the weighted variables, is distinctly a matter of good perceptual judgment, and I am calling this kind of subtle perception "sensing." Before we have the ability to sense plastic qualities, we do not know what to make of Fry's claim. Thus sensing impressions is a kind of subtle perception necessary to see the connection between a critic's reasons (placement of the figure) and his conclusion (verdict--the painting is imbalanced).[9] In summary, sensing always has to do with visual attention to multiple weighted variables. Sensibility involves a feeling for weighted perceptual variables while sensitivity is to a single aspect or phenomenon. Sensitivity is not as contextual as sensibility. Also given the Perceptual and Subtlety Conditions in the definition of sensing, it follows that we might not be able to articulate either the variables (cues) or their weighting, but these cues and their weighting must be potentially articulable.

Since sensing involves a Subtlety Condition, the objects we sense can become more refined. Things we

once sensed in a shaky and uncertain way may become
detectable with certainty, and we then simply see
them. Friedlander can simply see that a painting
is a Cézanne, but I might just sense Cézanne's style.
Later it might become obvious to me that this painting
is a Cézanne. We are able to shift our sensing to different levels and even different objects as our ability
to sense increases. Subtlety is ability relative. This
emphasis on the dynamics of a developing sensibility
will be an important part of my theorizing about stages
and styles of an accomplished ability to sense, a sensibility. Great paintings provide us with endless possibilities for sensing new subtleties.

With experience, when we make a subtlety shift to
new objects or qualities in picture space, we may say
we now see qualities and objects we once sensed with
hesitation. In such claims, we must remember we are
using "see" in the somewhat stretched sense noted
above in the problem of the Perceptual Condition and
illusionistic qualities. But if it is clear to everyone that we are using "see" and "sense" with the qualification that we mean objects in picture space, it is
helpful to be able to contrast obvious qualities with
subtleties. We do say we see overlap of objects in
realistic works like Holbein's "Erasmus." But we
sense Erasmus' nature, the nature of the picture space,
etc. We have to learn to sense subtle difference in
kinds of spaces, for example, those of late Cézanne,
Synthetic Cubism and Analytical Cubism. A very skilled
viewer might be able to say with justification that he
could see these differences. Thus, with the qualifications given, we can contrast "see" and "sense" in relation to obvious and subtle qualities.

Ordinary sensibilities can work against sensibilities to paintings. Sometimes it is necessary to relax
or discount ordinary perceptual cues in order to visually experience or sense illusionistic qualities. When
we move in physical space, foreground objects move in
relation to background objects. We must discount this
cue in order to sense picture space. We have already
noticed the tolerance of "sense" with regard to illusionistic qualities such as the Müller-Lyer illusion.
But often "sense" means the heightening of ordinary
perceptual acuteness so that illusions would be detected and avoided. Someone with a good sense of direction or distance knows how to discount misleading cues.
Sensing in this second sense would make sensing in the
illusionistic sense not operate. Certainly someone

with a good sense of depth, or anyone except someone very deficient visually, would see that a painting is flat, yet we also say we can sense the depth of the picture space. We must learn to discount certain cues and emphasize others. Certain ordinary visual abilities can be carried over to painting while others must be bracketed. In sensing a painting, the two kinds of sensing must not work against each other.

3) <u>The Selective Knowledge Condition</u>. The phrase "Selective Knowledge Condition" is meant to emphasize that sensing presupposes only certain kinds of perceptual knowledge and experience and other kinds of knowledge are excluded. This condition implies, in the spirit of common sensism, that one accumulates the knowledge necessary to sense something by encountering and acquiring experience with that thing. The Selective Knowledge Condition in a way is the negative counterpart of the Perceptual Condition. Thus it means that we can actually <u>perceive</u> an extensive range of meanings of things apart from cultural traditions such as traditions of symbolism.

3') Sensing impressions of paintings requires <u>only</u> a background of visual normalcy. What I mean by a background of visual normalcy is the extensive knowledge, gained in seeing in ordinary motor activities, of the relation between how things look and how they are. This background of visual normalcy will be characterized more fully in Chapter IX, and in connection with this characterization a theory of natural signs will be developed. In a preliminary way, this much can be said: A background of visual normalcy is exploited in creating impressions on basically two levels. Cues that excite visual normalcy in creating illusions are often used to set up a painting world. A painting world is the painting viewed so as to realize its physical and apparent qualities. For example, texture is an ordinary cue to distance, and painters use texture to create a world of picture space. At the second level, there is much carry-over of ordinary modes of attention and sensibility to objects in picture space (See qualifications in Chapter VI). The interpretation of caricature, for example, may require the same sort of sense of character which we attribute to persons in ordinary life. Neither level of exploiting visual normalcy requires any knowledge of symbolism or knowledge of historical events on the part of the viewer. The Selective Knowledge Condition means ordinary motor activities provide the viewer with the limited kind of knowledge needed to sense certain qualities in paintings.

The Selective Knowledge Condition expresses the sort of limitation of the viewer's knowledge a painter or critic must accept with the decline of knowledge of mythological, religious and historical subjects. As emphasized in the previous chapter, a painter or critic can no longer expect the viewer to have a knowledge of symbolism or to have an imagination warmed with the best products of ancient and modern poetry. Bell said we need bring only a sense of form, color and three dimensional space to a painting, but this is far too limited a range of ordinary sensibilities. Expressionistic and naturalistic paintings require other sensibilities such as a sense of emotive tone or a sense of character. The passage from Fry expressing a cross-cultural basis for the emotive elements of design suggests a theory of natural signs.[10] Also I reemphasize that contrary to Fry and Bell, my theory of sensing is not meant to disparage symbolism and the importance of literature, religion and myth for painting. In supporting his iconographic interpretations, Panofsky continually employs, and expressly theorizes about, sensibility to natural signs. Sensibility is just a different kind of ability and knowledge than that recommended by Reynolds.

The Selective Knowledge Condition is not only meant negatively, that is to exclude certain sorts of knowledge from sensing, but to emphasize other knowledge, namely visual knowledge. With the easy availability of prints, wide travel, the museum with large bodies of works on view, and the development of art history, with the concept of visual style, the viewer is expected to have a visual knowledge of many paintings. The Selective Knowledge Condition is meant to capture this greater visual demand on the viewer.

Sensing impressions of paintings will always involve what I shall characterize below as the painting as a causally active field and the painting as containing natural signs. When this field and these signs are looked at in the proper terms of attention, they will realize themselves by appearing certain ways or giving certain impressions. These kinds of impressions will vary from visual optical ones, such as space, to expressionistic ones, such as emotive impressions of faces. We have already seen in Ruskin and Baudelaire examples of the meaning of abstract elements of art being used to reinforce the meaning of the subject matter.

To move beyond the conditions defining sensing, I repeat that having good judgment or having sensibility is an <u>ability</u>, in contrast to occasional sensing. But <u>occasional</u> sensing satisfies the above conditions. Below I discuss ways in which the model of learning to sense or the model for refining our attention can be seated or ingrained as an ability (Chapter VI). This characterization will be a characterization of the ability to sense in contrast to an occasional sensing. There will be some special problems about sensing in an aesthetic context because of the difficulty of deciding who has good judgment in an aesthetic context.

One may make universal or limited claims to have sensed something. My theory will explain the universality involved in claims such as "that painting gives a sense of space" or "one can sense space in that painting." Also explained are less universal claims such as "Chinese viewers can sense those brush gestures in a way I cannot." The explanation of how paintings work in terms of cues exciting a background of visual normalcy deals with cultural peculiarities in sensing. My theory also gives sense to the claim "the painting may not give you a sense of space, but it does me," for there are peculiarities in all our backgrounds of visual normalcy. The universal or limited claims involved in sensing will be covered in Chapter IX. Further, there is always really an implicit qualification on the universality in claims of sensing paintings to the effect that <u>one who knows how to sense picture space will</u> sense a space in that painting. My model of a visual act and concept of experience with elements of art in models, defining examples and other works covers the ability and experience in this implicit qualification.

The definition of sensing will be developed in three parts: 1) A theory about the act of visual attention, developed in my model of a visual act. 2) A theory about the object of attention, namely the painting as a causally active field. 3) A theory about weighted variables accumulated by experience with paintings. This third point is really a part of the causal field point, but is distinct enough in its emphasis to merit a separate listing. The emphasis most unique to my analysis, so far as I know, is the first one. The theory about the painting as a causally active field uses views about the relation of sign and signified in C. S. Pierce and Thomas Reid, and my "theory" of natural signs is perhaps not developed enough to be called a "theory". The third point about the weighting of variables is adapted from experimental findings on abilities such as space perception.

    I do not claim that the ordinary meaning of "sense" and "sensibility" <u>explicitly</u> includes the three main conditions defining sensing, but I do claim the theory of sensing is both consistent with the ordinary meaning and even in the spirit of the ordinary meaning. In going beyond the ordinary meaning of sensing, my <u>theory</u> of sensing is derived from theories of perception, especially those of J. J. Gibson, and from extensions I have made of action terminology to visual attention. I will often speak of the theory as being plausible, and the data I relate it to is the self-knowledge we have of what happens to our seeing when we read critics and art historians and become more experienced with paintings. Also, the data I claim the theory covers is the nature of arguments about specific paintings in criticism. Finally, I claim the theory is adequate to what is known experimentally about vision. Thus, my argument will typically sometimes refer to the meaning of "sense" and "sensibility," and of course this is a procedure used by ordinary language philosophers. But my argument will even more often go beyond the ordinary meaning and claim <u>plausibility</u> in terms of the data mentioned. This mixture of meaning and plausibility seems to me a reasonable procedure when one is dealing with an ordinary concept which lacks precision and about which there is a considerable body of theoretical findings which can be used to give the ordinary concept precision.

    In the next four chapters (III-VI) I develop the Perceptual and Subtlety Conditions, culminating in a characterization of sensing as an ability (VI). Chapter IX completes the Selective Knowledge Condition.

ENDNOTES

[1] Vesey distinguishes optical illusions, those which occur purely physically due to phenomena such as bending of light rays, from visual illusions. The Müller-Lyer illusion is visual because it involves the nature of the eye and is not merely optical and physical interactions. See Godfrey Vesey, Perception (Garden City, N. Y.: Anchor Books, 1971), p. 11. Both optical and visual illusions, however, have a causal base in the optical context or the eye, and both are distinct from delusions or imaginings which have no basis in the optical context or nature of the eye. What I am calling "impressions" covers both visual and optical illusions, though most of my examples are visual ones.

[2] It is inappropriate to use "sense" when one can plainly see something, as one does not sense a man in Holbein's "Erasmus of Rotterdam." See the Subtlety Condition below for the contrast between seeing and sensing.

[3] Roderick M. Chisholm, Theory of Knowledge, Second ed. (Englewood Cliffs, N. J.: Prentice-Hall, 1977).

[4] Paintings cause impressions in several senses: 1) The most direct sense of causation is when the physiology of the eye causes some impression, such as the working of complementary colors. 2) A somewhat milder sense of causation is when deep seated scanning habits, such as those of reading, cause some impression, as reading habits are known to affect the way compositions are "read." 3) A still milder sense of an impression being caused by a painting is when some object in picture space is similar enough to some ordinary object to borrow plastic and emotive qualities from the ordinary objects. Objects in picture space are animated, to greater or less degree, by the visual looks of ordinary objects. I consider all three examples instances in which a painting directly causes an impression. It is not possible to be any more precise about the nature of the causes of impressions given the present state of our knowledge of the eye and brain.

[5] Sibley, pp. 421-50.

[6] Paul Ziff, "Reasons in Art Criticism," in Margolis, ed., Philosophy Looks at the Arts (New York: Charles Scribner's Sons, 1962), pp. 163-64. Originally in I. Shaffler, ed., Philosophy and Education (Boston: Allyn and Bacon, 1958), pp. 219-236.

[7] J. L. Austin, Philosophical Papers, ed. J. O. Urmson and G. J. Warnock (Oxford: The Clarendon Press, 1962), pp. 74-75.

[8] Roger Fry, Transformations: Critical and Speculative Essays on Art (London: Chatto and Windus, 1926), pp. 16-18.

[9] There is a kind of circle here in that one cannot evaluate what a critic says until one already has the kind of sensibility one is learning from that critic, but I will argue that the circle is not vicious.

[10] Fry, Vision and Design, pp. 34-35.

CHAPTER III

ORDINARY VISUAL ACTS

In this chapter I develop a <u>general</u> theory of visual acts and develop the model of <u>visual</u> attention. Since sensing, as I define it, contains a Perceptual Condition and a Subtlety Condition, sensing as a visual ability must be related to the more general concept of visual attention. In Chapter IV, I apply the model to actual examples <u>from critics</u>, and I argue that learning to sense from critics can plausibly be interpreted as learning to look at paintings in terms of the model of a visual act given in this chapter. Sensing, as I understand it, is a sophisticated visual ability which is developed by learning how to look at a painting in the proper units and centers of attention. Thus, the general theory of visual attention in this chapter is not a digression. The model of a visual act of attention introduced here is the way I develop the Perceptual Condition and the Subtlety Condition in the definition of sensing.

A comment is needed on the distinction between acts and activities. I will understand acts as defined by intention, following Anscombe.[1] Our acts are described by honest answers to questions about what we are doing. Intentions are formulated verbally, and are commonly called reasons for actions. Acts do not cover, of course, the full range of purposive human doings. I use "activities" to cover purposive activities in a broader sense, where each part of the activity need not involve a conscious purpose. A skill is a good example not covered by the concept of an act. Visual exploring in sensing is another. A skill may be learned analytically from verbal instruction, and my model of a visual act analyzes how we learn to sense. In the process of learning, one may have reasons for each detail of the act. But with practice, of course, we can gradually relegate some action which we had to constantly supervise by reason and correction to the smooth flow of bodily practice. Our mind and intentions then are freed for the subtleties of the context in which the skill is used. At the moment of employing the skill acquired, a description of the <u>conscious</u> intention would fall far short of the full range of purpose shown. I think we would thus say that employing a skill is more like a purposive activity than just an act. There is a reservoir of ability drawn on that is purposive, but one is no longer conscious of the detail of learning the skill. A developed sensibility is like lessons absorbed, having the flow of a skilled action, and thus sensing a painting is an activity. As in other activities conscious thoughts are involved, but also the funded experience of viewing is involved. An astronomer practicing averted vision in order to see a dim galaxy is practicing a purposive activity. But, given this distinction, it is more convenient to use "act of viewing" than "activity of skilled viewing." Most literally, what viewing a painting is like is engaging in a skilled visual activity for a span of time. For convenience it is easier to refer to the whole span of a viewing as "an act of viewing" instead of "a span of an activity of skilled viewing." The latter is, however, a closer description of what I think sensibility is like. Sensing is really employing acquired abilities over a span of time in viewing a painting. The purpose of my model of a visual act is mainly to show that visual attention can be considered a purposively developed activity, and thus it falls, at least partially, in the area of ability which can be intentionally acquired or developed. The model of a visual act emphasizes the possibilities of refined perception as a part of sensibility.

Model of a Visual Act

Visual attention to the color of some object, when skilled and complete, is a visual act learned from a redundant complex of verbal categories, spatial reference aiders, techniques, devices and even eye techniques; and, for convenience, I shall serialize these redundant elements of visual attention into object-side, intermediate, and eye-side elements of attention. (By "object-side" I mean the particular physical object, specifically a painting, as described or characterized, the verbal description or characterization being essential to define the object of attention.[2] By "eye-side" I mean eye directions such as focus, scan, blur, or squint the eyes. Also I use "eye-side" loosely to cover head-side directions such as "stand back so far you cannot recognize the objects if you want to look at the color scheme." By "intermediate" I mean techniques, devices and aids imposed between the eyes and the object in order to aid the relevant mode of attention.) The idea here is that in attending we use our eyes in certain ways, sometimes assisted by devices, on the object of attention. During the process of learning, the lessons, verbal and otherwise, must be assimilated into a smooth and practiced visual act, like other skilled acts, with the subsequent development of what I call perceptual refinement abilities--abilities such as discrimination, sensitivity and acuity.[3] The visual astronomer practices averted vision, the holding of the fovea several degrees off the object of attention, so as to increase the eye's sensitivity to light. One's sensitivity can often be extended by more than a stellar magnitude through this eye technique, and it is amazing how much more detail of dim celestial objects an astronomer can see as compared to an untrained observer of the same visual ability. Analogously, I shall argue that one can practice modes of attention appropriate to paintings, and, with practice, the act becomes smooth and efficient through the development of perceptual refinement abilities which I will call sensibilities. Of course, there are important differences, too, between a visual skill like averted vision and sensitively perceiving a painting. I shall emphasize these differences in saying one does not look at aspects and features of nature in the same way that one does at elements of art. I introduce the model of a visual act in the order of object, intermediate, and eye-side elements of visual attention.

Descriptions, Ostensive Defining and the Object of Attention

White makes this remark about descriptions and the object of attention: "One cannot give one's attention in any way to anything without knowing that one is attending and also knowing under some description what one is attending to."[4] I dispute the claim that one cannot attend without "knowing under some description what one is attending to." Animals can be trained to attend to aspects of objects, such as a color which releases food. I think we would normally say a rat or pigeon so trained had learned to attend to a color or learned to notice color without saying the animal knew under some description what he was attending to. Of course, one cannot specify or define a mode of attention without giving some description of the object of attention. One cannot answer what one is attending to without a description. But specifying a mode of attention is different from attending in some sensory mode.

43

Further, I think artists learn to attend to most element of their art by the practice of painting. Often they cannot give a description of what they are attending to. It is widely thought--and I think truly thought--that one can learn to see a painting from drawing and other painting activities, and in fact painters' sensibilities are developed mainly by painting acts. The painter has a dim intuition of a visual possibility, paints works which begin to exploit this possibility, in the process of which his sensibility is refined, from which new realizations he can visualize or intuit further into this possibility, from which further realizations of the idea are achieved, etc. Cézanne's torturous attempts to realize his vision well illustrate this dialectic. Reid nicely put it: "Every artist acquires an eye as well as a hand in his own profession. His eye becomes skilled in perceiving, no less than his hand in executing, what belongs to his employment."[5] (Wittgenstein noted that non-verbal behavior shows "categories" of attention which are essential in teaching words. The child in crying sometimes shows he is attending to a pain, and it is easiest, and perhaps only possible, to teach "pain" in such a context. The verbal expression replaces crying.[6] Analogously, language-games develop nonverbal modes of attention, "categories" of attention, which should be capitalized on in teaching language.) Further, even though we usually <u>learn</u> to see in certain terms verbally, we can eventually develop an integrity and independence in our practiced visual acts. Later we may notice visual subtleties without verbal cues. Even though we learn to see in certain terms, <u>modes</u> of seeing can be non-verbal forms of noticing. Noticing means that one is or was consciously occupied with a thing considered in a certain way, but being consciously so occupied does not necessarily mean a verbally articulated or verbally directed form of consciousness. We can <u>visually</u> explore and notice subtleties in a painting. In fact, this is what sensibility is.

Even though a description is not a necessary condition of attention, I am basically interested in attention which is verbally acquired. In a sense, successful ostensive defining of visual terms is a sufficient condition of visual attention. Generally attention can be related to ostensive defining as understood by Wittgenstein.[7] Many techniques such as pointing to or directing one's glance towards the object may also be used to draw or direct attention. The most important similarity between ostensive teaching and attention is that ostensive defining is a way of getting the child to <u>see what</u>

is meant. Ostensive defining shows the intentionality or directionality involved in visual attention and reference.[8] Ostensive teaching, as well as ostensive defining, requires a sort of sensory uptake on the object of attention. (This sensory uptake will be important in the different kinds and styles of uptakes involved in various successful verbal acts of critics.) I emphasize that though a child can visually identify sepia without even being able to say "sepia" (just as an animal can), we would not say being able to visually attend to a color or being able to pick out a color is sufficient to see what we mean by "sepia." A necessary condition of seeing what we mean, in contrast to visual attention, is seeing an object as verbally described. We have to be trying to mean something and be taken to mean something for someone to see what we mean.[9] It is mainly through verbal functions that knowledge of critics and painters gets attached, so to speak, to the painting as a visual object. We recall Isenberg's epigram that the purpose of criticism is to bring about communication at the level of the senses, which can be described as getting us to see what is meant.[10] Since the visual array in a painting, unlike ordinary visual arrays, was made for a purpose, and thus was made to be seen in certain ways, the critic's getting us to see what he means should be sympathetic to what the painter meant the painting to do. In a sense, we get to see what the painter meant the painting to do.

When acts of visual attention are learned from verbal acts such as ostensive defining, the attention has the same sort of generality as is involved in verbal functions such as referring to an aspect of a particular or describing a particular. Wittgenstein's points about pain, as a something about which nothing could be said, I think can be extended.[11] If I say, "look at X," where X means some aspect of a particular, and this aspect can in no way be described or related to other aspects, we could never be sure we were meaning the same thing by "X." There could be nothing more than bare spatial indication of the thing, perhaps by pointing, but there could be no certainty we were attending to the same aspect of it, nor even that what we were attending to should be called an "aspect." On the contrary, acts learned through verbal acts must have an essential generality.[12]

A second, aesthetic, argument for the generality of visual acts extends the above argument to the stronger claim that elements of art worth attending to in a

skilled mode must be embodied in at least several works.
(The above private language argument allows the possibility, now being excluded, that a combination of publicly definable terms applies to only one object.) A painter cannot expect us to learn a mode of vision--an ingrained visual ability--which works against other paintings or is not helpful in perceiving other paintings. The balance between intensity and extensity of experience in aesthetic perception, though flexible and shifting, would be destroyed by terms applicable to only one work. A related argument is that significant, and even original, elements of art must be embodied in at least several works. Critical characterizations, descriptions, interpretations, and explanations usually suggest a general mode of sensing. The critic usually means that the terms of an explanation or characterization can be applied to a class of works of some extension--say, other works by the painter in the same period, the whole corpus of works by a painter, works of the same school, works of the same period, etc. Sensibilities, then, are typical visual acts in the sense of being about a class of some extension and in being specified in terms of elements of the works of this class. All my remarks are about visual acts of some generality, though the visual acts may involve odd and hyphenated modes of attention such as color-schemes-considered-from-an-expressionistic point of view.[13]

Even though acts of attention have the sort of generality noted, noticing, which completes the act of attention, is a distinctive kind of occurrence. The generality of the visual act is the mode in which one sees, the degree to which the mode is habitual and like a skill, and noticing is an occurrence within that mode. Ordinarily, as well as here, we distinghish attention as a general state of expectancy from visual noticing. One may pay attention, and yet not notice something. Attentiveness is a preparation for acts of seeing, sensing, and noticing. Learning to attend to a certain kind of object is a purposive activity which is hopefully completed by noticing what was in question about that object. Attention is related to the general states of being attentive, being observant, being alert. Sometimes one may even notice something without being attentive, as in "I inadvertently saw____," or "my eye was drawn to____." But even though ordinary noticing can take place without attention, almost involuntarily, noticing a subtlety almost never takes place without preparation, and thus the oddity of an inexperienced person saying "I suddenly noticed the Cubistic space of Pollock." One does not inadvertently notice the details of a dim galaxy or the spatial structure of Pollock.

Even though I have distinguished attention from noticing, and even though one may attend without noticing and conversely, there is a general purposive relationship between acts of attention and noticing, and paradigms of attention involve noticing or seeing the quality in question. Thus learning to sense in certain terms is analogous to learning to attend to qualities one expects to notice. The terms of attention, in sophisticated sensing, direct attention to relevant units, places, etc., where there might be sensitive up-take in noticing.

An example of other verbal equipment a child has to have to master attention to color is what we might call part-whole reference aiders. "Part" is a covering term for any number of spatial units--fragments, parts, pieces, segments, areas, planes, regions, blended areas, brush strokes, blobs, drips, etc. These combine, of course, into very different kinds of wholes. Aspect terms such as "color" and "texture" essentially include certain kinds of part-whole units. Of course, we usually combine part-whole reference with attention to an aspect of something. We look at areas of color, sections of line, rays of light--each of the supplemental reference aiders ("area," "section," "ray") showing the kind of part unit appropriate to the aspect. In fact, aspects of objects are just certain kinds of part-wholes. Color is one kind of part-whole, texture another. In general, a child who constantly referred to a piece of color or who did not show that he knew line occurred in sections and sweeps would not be said to understand the concept of color or line respectively.

In summary, even though verbal descriptions are not necessary conditions of attending to an object of attention, correct taking of a verbal function, such an ostensive defining, is a sufficient condition for attending to an object as specified, and this sort of direction of attention through verbal situations is the main sort emphasized here. It is only through verbal functions such as describing, characterizing, or explaining with regard to the object of attention that critics get us to see in terms appropriate to the purposes of a painting. However, after practice, we may visually explore and notice subtleties without verbally articulating the object of attention. Further, ostensive defining assures that visual attention will have generality, for we cannot ostensively define a peculiar or private object or a private aspect of an object.

The phrase "object of attention" (and other senses of object in an intentional sense) is notoriously ambiguous. One sense relevant to the above discussion is the object-with-description, call this the verbal intentional object. Another sense of "object of attention," also emphasized above, is the visual object, the visual units, centers of attention, groupings of objects, etc. I call this sense the visual intentional object, and my arguments concerning the independence of sensing from the verbal (and other) ways one learns to sense concern the visual intentional object. Verbal functions considered in themselves are, strictly speaking, like the intermediate aids discussed next; but when the verbal function is successful, given all the various ways in which they can be successful, the verbal intentional object is completed by the visual intentional object, that is, one senses the painting as described, characterized, etc. One notices or has already noticed the painting as described, characterized, etc. I shall use "object of attention" where the distinction between the verbal intentional object and visual intentional object is not important.

Intermediate Aids to Attention

"Intermediate aids" here means the devices and techniques we can place between the eye and the object of attention in order to perfect attention. Even our gestures can be made suitable to the aspect of the object we are referring to. A generalized gesture to a vaguely bounded area is appropriate to an area of color, while a sweeping gesture pointing to a sweep of line can express the nature and tempo of the sweep of a line. A good museum lecturer does not point to color, line, or texture in the same way. One does not point to pieces, sections, and areas in the same way. A child who referred to a "piece of color" would possibly also make inappropriate gestures in ostensively defining color for others. There is, of course, redundancy in spatial reference aiders and gestures. Reference aiders often indicate the kind of "edge" (area versus section, for example) the object has or the kind of edge the focus of attention will impose. Also intermediate between the eye and object are techniques such as cupping one's hands so as to isolate a color from

its context and from other aspects such as shape or
outline. Of course, there is redundancy between cupping one's hands, spatial aiders such as "area,"
gestures, and aspection terms such as "color." Cupping
one's hands is a good illustration of the difference
between reference and ostensive defining and visual attention, for it goes beyond the requirements for clear
reference and is a part of the <u>visual skill</u> of attending to color. Another example of an intermediate aid
which can be used in mastering the skill of looking at
color is a piece of paper with a hole in it. Such aids,
of course, function similarly to cupping one's hands.
Intermediate aids are quasi-conceptual and quasi-
visual. Symbols, arrows and gestures of pointing are
on the conceptual or linguistic side while aids such
as a piece of paper with a hole in it are more visual.
Intermediate aids, for example, drawn overlays demon-
strating how a painting's composition works, will show
even more clearly the quasi-conceptual/quasi-visual
status of intermediate aids.

Eye-Side Aspects of Attention

Completely on the eye-side are such techniques as
blurring one's eyes in order to see color. One can
practice acute vision, foveating, on an area of texture, or one can practice acute vision of a whole field.
We can practice at least acute or blurred vision on an
area or whole field.

In summary, from the object-side to the eye-side
there are redundant and overlapping verbal means, gestures, and techniques which are employed in skilled
attention to color, for example. Any one element in
acquiring this visual skill, of course, can be omitted
since the elements are redundant, but a number of in-
capacities lessens visual skill and makes us reluctant
to say one has mastered the skill of attending to color.
There is a special place, however, for the verbal intentional object in defining the mode of attention.
Thus <u>how</u> one attends, in contrast to what one attends
to, is not definitive of a mode of attention. There
are analogous redundancies in ordinary referring and
ostensive defining. The use one makes of various elements of attention (including eye-side directions,
pointing aiders such as "area," "region," "mass,"
"section" and object specification) can show category
sensitivity or insensitivity. Blurring the eyes,
standing back too far to recognize subject matter,

masking the outline with a paper with a hole in it, looking in terms of areas of color, ignoring the outline, texture, shading--each of these show, in different kinds of techniques and modes of attention, our belief about the nature of color. Color is a spread-out visual phenomenon different from texture, shape and outline, or, more precisely, our attention to color treats it as a spread-out visual phenomenon. Color occurs in the units of the thing it is the color of, but to isolate color from other aspects we try to attend to areas or regions of color. (In a sense I am here agreeing with Aristotle that a secondary category such as quality can be treated as having its own substantial nature.) When one uses appropriate verbal categories, techniques of gesture and devices, one shows a category normal mode of attention to color. The verbal instruction "Look at a piece of color," and non-verbal techniques of looking at pieces do not show such category normalcy for color.

Attention to a painting often requires category abnormalities. One has to look at the shape of holes in some of DuBuffet's paintings, and one has to look at planes of color in Cézanne. Very often, in fact, painters want to change or refine our means of reference. Notice Ben Shan's book title The Shape of Content. Such category changes or crossings affect attention on the eye-side and object-side.[14]

Attention to a color or attention to a dim galaxy are both rather specialized discriminative abilities which can be developed somewhat by practice of eye techniques, devices, etc. I will call increases in sensitivity, discrimination, or acuity increases in discriminative abilities. It is obvious that discriminative abilities in this narrow sense are of rather limited application in learning to sense qualities of paintings, though they are not irrelevant. So I now extend the concept of perceptual refinement abilities beyond discriminative abilities, thus completing the concept of sensibility. A main difference between an ordinary act of attention, such as seeing color, and sensing elements of art is that the creative nature of painting makes continual demands for new descriptions of the object of attention. This sort of category-flux was intimated above in remarks about oddities of reference involved in attending to planes of color or attending to shapes of holes. There is so much flux in how we attend to a painting that the ordinary redundancy and certainty given by various eye-side, intermediate, and object-side devices and techniques do not develop. Creative acts of vision and creative verbal acts are continually demanded of critics and viewers in order to attend to the proper object of attention. As I complete the analysis of sensing, seeing a painting begins to sound less like a literal set of visual skills and more like a creative art of seeing.

ENDNOTES

[1] G. E. M. Anscombe, *Intention* (Oxford: B. Blackwell, 1963), pp. 9-11; 83-87.

[2] I distinguish descriptions or characterizations being essential to *define* a mode of attention from their being essential for there to *be* a mode of attention. I deny that verbal concepts are necessary for attention simpliciter. See below.

[3] James J. Gibson, *The Senses Considered as Perceptual Systems* (London: 1968), p. 51. "We can now suppose that the perceptual systems develop perceptual skills, with some analogy to the way in which the behavioral systems develop performatory skills."

[4] Allan R. White, *Attention* (Oxford: B. Blackwell, 1964), p. 2.

[5] Thomas Reid, *Essays on the Intellectual Powers*, p. 306.

[6] Ludwig Wittgenstein, *Philosophical Investigations*, trans. G. E. M. Anscombe (New York: Macmillan, 1960), sec. 244.

[7] *Ibid.*, secs. 1-9; 28-30.

[8] This purposive relationship between attention and noticing is what I mean by "intentionality." Also "intentionality" means the directionality of attention on some object. My sense of "intentionality" is closer to Husserl's sense (Edmund Husserl, *Ideas: General Introduction to Pure Phenomenology*, trans. W. R. Boyce Gibson [London: George Allen and Unwin, 1958], p. 346). than to Chisholm's sense (Roderick M. Chisholm, *Perceiving: A Philosophical Study* [Ithaca, New York: Cornell University Press, 1957], pp. 168-85).

[9] H. P. Grice, "Meaning," *The Philosophical Review*, 66, No. 3 (1957), pp. 377-88.

[10] Arnold Isenberg, "Critical Communication," *The Philosophical Review*, 68 (July, 1949), p. 336.

[11] Wittgenstein, sec. 293f.

[12] I realize that the private language argument is debatable. Wittgenstein makes at least four or five different suggestions about what he means to claim, and I consider some of the suggestions definitely wrong. I do accept his argument that a sound or sign cannot function <u>in the full sense</u> as a word in ordinary language if it refers to some private and indescribable object. But Wittgenstein seems to suggest that we cannot attend to a private object before we have learned the linguistic act of ostensive defining. I am explicitly denying this in emphasizing non-verbal and preverbal ways we direct attention. As indicated, Wittgenstein himself in other places emphasizes prelinguistic attention, as in the example of learning "I am in pain."

[13] The <u>kinds</u> of classes involved in general terms can be very different. Throughout the book, I shall use as my example seeing in terms of <u>aesthetic positions</u>, such as purism, expressionism, or naturalism. The corpus of work of a painter is a completely different sort of class. A style of painting is a different kind of class still. Our experience with painting can be in terms of at least these kinds of classes. Often our experience with painting will involve <u>two</u> kinds of classes, as we may be experienced in viewing paintings in terms of purism, and may also be experienced with Cézanne's work. I believe my model of a visual act can be adapted to kinds of classes other than classing in terms of aesthetic positions, my main example.

[14] We might note here that original elements of art which demand strange verbal complexes are in a sense visual metaphors. Original visual elements may create new kinds of space, open up expressive possibilities or give insight into some subject. Such original elements of art are metaphorical in that they are both like and unlike their ordinary counterparts. A critic has to discover creative verbal functions, with category crossings, to express the visual metaphors. Not just any bizarre combination visually or verbally is a metaphor--insight or some new expressive possibility must be opened up.

CHAPTER IV

VISUAL ACTS AND ELEMENTS OF ART

There is an important qualification that has to be made to extend my model of a visual act to paintings. Paintings are obviously very rich and <u>complex contexts</u>, and thus learning to look at a painting is very different from learning to attend to a color. We might say color is one dimensional (some systems of classification, of course, break it down into several variables such as hue, saturation, and intensity), and thus the purpose of the visual act of attending to color is mainly to decontextualize, that is, to learn to discount texture, shape, peculiarities of light, etc. Even the most minimal painting, however, is multidimensional in the sense that there is interaction of several sorts of things. Thus learning to see a painting is learning to attend to numerous interacting variables. There is at least as much re-contextualizing as there is decontextualizing. How one knows how to weigh these interacting variables in a rich context will be a main problem to be dealt with in my theory of sensibility.

This chapter and the model of learning to attend from the last chapter show how we take passages from critics <u>pedagogically</u>, that is how we take passages from critics when we are trying to <u>learn</u> to sense in the terms of attention of the critic. This emphasis means, of course, that we must have some reason for wanting to learn to sense in these terms other than our as yet non-existent sensibility in those sorts of terms. Critics often give arguments for the terms of their criticism, and we may find the arguments convincing. We often pick a critic on the basis of his reputation or perhaps because he favorably discusses painters we like. Initially, we are not able, because of lacking ability to sense in the relevant term, to find a critic's descriptions, characterization, explanations and interpretations sound, plausible, distorting, etc. This chapter thus deals with learning to attend in the relevant units and modes of attention so that, with practice of the terms of attention on many paintings, we may eventually have the ability to sense in the terms of the critic chosen. Also this chapter deals only with the redistribution of attention so as to learn to sense in well established terms of criticism, namely those of purism, expressionism and naturalism. The special problems of sensing in terms of attention appropriate to original art will arise shortly.

Eye-side

Actual eye directions, such as focus or blur the eyes, are relatively rare in critics. Baudelaire does advise standing back from a painting so far that one cannot recognize the subject matter,[1] and the advice to blur one's eyes is sometimes given as an aid to seeing color schemes. But eye directions alone, without reference to the object of attention, are relatively rare in critics. There are many claims about where one should direct one's eyes or where one's eyes are drawn, as examples below show, but these are eye directions in terms of the object of attention, and not merely eye directions to focus, blur or squint the eyes. One may follow the latter directions without mentioning the object of attention.

Intermediate Visual Aids to Direct Attention

The redirection of attention in terms of purism, expressionism and naturalism has a spatial element. There are new centers of attention, and these can be spatially indicated by pointing or by drawing arrows. There are new groupings of objects, and both inter-thing lines leading or drawing attention and inter-thing gestalts formed by outlines of several things are often exploited by painters. Again these have a spatial dimension. An inter-thing gestalt can be traced by pointing or by drawing the inter-thing gestalt. Thus learning to attend to paintings, which is redirecting our attention so we can sense a painting's qualities, involves new centers of attention, new groupings of objects and new kinds of objects. Of course not all this redirection of attention can be accomplished by spatial aids (such as pointing or diagraming) alone, and we have mentioned, as Wittgenstein emphasized, that it was naive to think that a spatial indicator, such as pointing, was self-evident apart from some form of life and shared body of knowledge of behavioral conventions. In learning some aesthetic mode of attention, we must attend to new things, which can be spatially indicated, and new aspects of these things, which cannot be spatially indicated. We can point to things but not to plastic qualities of things, for example. We can point to a thing but not to its color. The new kinds of objects of attention emphasized by purism, expressionism and naturalism can be attended to only with the aid of verbal functions such as describing, characterizing, interpreting and explaining. Thus full direction of attention appropriate to various kinds of sensing requires spatial aids with descriptions, characterizations, interpretations and explanations. Still critics do make extensive use of spatial aids in teaching us to sense paintings, and I will deal in some detail with one kind of spatial aid, the drawn overlay. I will temporarily describe drawn overlays in isolation from verbal functions and conventions of a form of life, though of course they would not really work without this background.

Intermediate aids are widely used, and, in the way in which I present them as drawn overlays, there is an implicit reference to the painting as an object of attention. I have mentioned intermediate aids as widely varied as gestures or a piece of paper with a hole in it. By a drawn overlay I mean a drawing on some transparent material which can be superimposed on the painting. Such overlays function analogously to gestures in front of a painting. Both gestures and overlays redistribute the viewer's attention or regroup objects of attention (as figures related in a triangular form in Leonardo's "Madonna of the Rocks"). Drawn overlays also accomplish what one could achieve by actually drawing over a painting. Critics and art historians sometimes do use a print which is drawn over to illustrate a painting's basic compositional structure, the objects the eye is lead or drawn to, etc. Obviously, verbal functions are the main ways attention is redistributed. Instead of drawing the triangle around the figures in the Leonardo, one might simply say it has a triangular structure.

Drawn overlays are simply graphic illustrations of how much redirection of attention is involved in sensing. They also illustrate typical visual units required in different kinds of sensing. Drawn overlays have this advantage over similar verbal functions: The overlays are in visual units, and thus they can be used not only to make a claim about how a painting works, but also to exemplify the very units of the painting's working. Drawn overlays, when they have symbols on them such as arrows, are quasi-conceptual and quasi-visual. The triangular overlay that would illustrate the sort of inter-thing gestalt in the Leonardo is obvious. Fry makes this claim about Daumier's "Gar St. Lazare."

> The group to the right is the most plastically satisfactory of all, and the device of the box being lowered from the cab roof and carrying on the diagonal of the man's top-hat breaks for the first time the monotony of the horizontal line of heads.[2]

This drawn overlay (Figure 1) illustrates the inter-thing line formed by the box and the hat of the avaricious man. Ruskin, in analyzing Turner's "Pass of Fiado," gives his own sketch of the scene, and then shows the changes Turner made in order to capture or express "the full essence and soul of the scene."[3] One could use this drawn overlay (Figure 2) to illustrate the sorts of units of attention (masses in relation to the minute human subjects) involved in Ruskin's analysis. One could use this overlay (Figure 3) to emphasize the planes of color in Cézanne's "Mount St. Victoire." Direction of attention to areas of color, in contrast to planes of color, would call for an overlay with indistinctly bounded regions of color. One can use this overlay (Figure 4) to illustrate the tensions between planes of color in Hofmann's "Equipoise". The use of arrows to direct attention to expressively alive features of a person or situation, of course, could be extensive.

Not only do drawn overlays graphically illustrate the sort of redirection of attention needed to learn to sense or to refer to objects of attention in painting, but also drawn overlays can be considered illustrations of the visual units paintings generate to be overlaid on the world. We can learn to see landscapes as planes of color, and Goodman has vigorously reminded us of the articulating function of paintings and other artistic symbolic schemes.[4] Thus, drawn overlays not only show how we redirect our attention to sense a painting's qualities, but also how we might recenter attention on some new qualities in our ordinary visual fields.

Daumier "Gare St. Lazare"
Figure 1

Turner "Pass of Faido"
Figure 2

Cézanne "Mount Saint-Victoire, seen from the Colline Des Lauves"

Figure 3

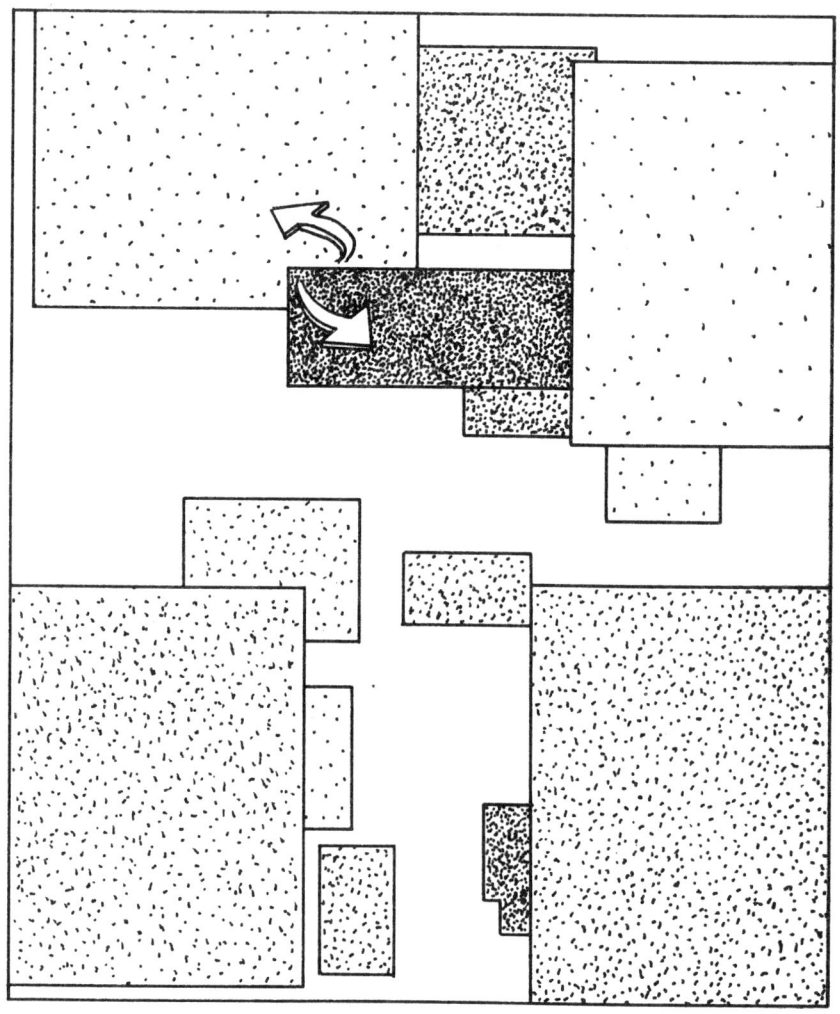

Hofmann "Equipoise"

Figure 4

Verbal Aids to Direct Attention

There are, of course, many reasons why one cannot achieve reference or direction of attention by spatial aids alone. At the very least, we can more efficiently refer to something or direct attention to something by using verbal functions with spatial diagrams instead of using spatial aids alone. The examples already cited from critics illustrate this fuller direction of attention. Fry refers to the group to the right in the Daumier being "the most plastically satisfactory of all . . . ." He does not achieve this reference by spatial indication alone, but he verbally directs our attention to plastic qualities of the group on the right. Ruskin spoke of the soul of the scene, and he showed by descriptions and diagrams changes Turner made in order to capture the deeper truth of the landscape.

A critic can historically place a painter by describing, interpreting, characterizing and explaining his works. One cannot achieve such historical placing by diagrams and intermediate aids alone. Critics do often characterize painters by placing them in terms of historical styles, but we need not digress into the very difficult subject of visual styles. Another advantage of verbal functions of critics in contrast to bare spatial indication in a painting is that critics can place two paintings in comparison in terms of their total range of connotations. I found this passage from Clark wonderfully descriptive of the elusive difference between Gothic nudes and nudes from the Italian tradition.

> Roots and bulbs, pulled up into the light, give us for a moment a feeling of shame. They are pale, defenseless, unself-supporting. They have the formless character of life that has been protected and oppressed. In the darkness their slow, biological gropings have been the contrary of the quick, resolute movements of free creatures, bird, fish, or dancer, flashing through a transparent medium, and have made them baggy, scraggy, and indeterminate. Looking at a group of naked figures in a Gothic painting or minature, we experience the same sensation.[5]

Another advantage of a critic's use of verbal functions, and the most important one considered here, is that critics thereby verbally tell us what aspects of things to consider. Wittgenstein noted that if I point to a thing, that thing could be considered, among indefinite other possibilities, in terms of aspects such as color, shape or texture. Spatial indication alone does not tell us which of these to attend to. Pointing is not self evident. If I do not know sepia is a color, the ostensive definition "this is sepia" will not work.[6]

Instead of developing Wittgenstein's concept of aspects, I emphasize that critics give us certain terms of attention. "Terms" mean each selective dimension of things in picture space which purists, expressionists and naturalists invite us to attend to. Fry speaks of plastic qualities, and in the example cited he seems to mean composition in terms of volumes and masses. Purists often also employ terms emphasizing composition in terms of color or light. Rhythms also can be considered as relevant to plastic qualities. Naturalists such as Ruskin consider paintings in very different terms. Ruskin thought painters should try to capture nature, the soul of scenes. Thus he considered both subject matter and abstract elements of art in terms of the idea of nature conveyed. To have a complete naturalism of course one has to have an idea of _true_ nature, as Ruskin claims to have, but the definition of true nature goes beyond sensing, even though sensing is employed in determining what idea about nature is being expressed by a particular painting. Expressionism is done in different terms still. Often serious emotions such as melancholiness are emphasized. Also expressionists often emphasize the painter himself, as in Baudelaire's statement that the artist uses nature as a dictionary in order to express his own nature.

There are, of course, any number of _kinds_ of classes which one may impose on a painting, but I am using "terms" to mean paintings considered from the point of view of some aesthetic position. The practice of considering paintings in terms of visual styles shows the very different kind of classing of art historians. Thus I develop my theory of sensing in terms of aesthetic positions, though I have not denied other forms of sensing are relevant, say to the way art historians group paintings. Friedlander no doubt employs his ability to sense in trying to determine if a painting genuinely shows the style of some painter. Thus "terms" here will mean the consideration of objects in picture space from the point of view of some aesthetic position, for example, puristic, expressionistic and naturalistic.

"Terms" as used here does not mean isolated words, though critics favor certain words and phrases, as Baudelaire likes to use "mélancholie." "Terms" include any words within a relatively close synonym range, as "plaintiff" is a word Baudelaire sometimes uses instead of melancholy. Further, any size linguistic unit can be in the same terms. Thus "terms" means any sort of linguistic unit which is typical of a certain aesthetic position or way of talking about a painting. If asked "In what terms did he criticize the painting?" natural answers would be naturalistic, expressionistic, or puristic. These positions or terms of habitual attention do not mean a critic uses certain words, but they do mean various sized linguistic units show an aesthetic position or point of view. It is quite easy to express the terms of attention in Baudelaire and Ruskin because both theorize extensively about the faculty (imagination) which is employed in the greatest art. When they use their basic terms ("imagination" or synonyms or larger linguistic units with the same meaning), the meaning and critical force of the terms is clear. In contemporary and less theoretical critics one often has to infer the critic's terms of criticism from his usage.

Terms are generalizable ways of looking at paintings, and thus they have the generality necessary for a visual act. If there is not some consistency or repetition of terms in a certain critic, I deny that that critic has an aesthetic position or terms of criticism. The justification of the generality in terms of looking at a painting is simply the fact that there is some communality of purposes and achievements among painters. Even when the relationship among painters is loose (perhaps with Pagiolli we should say modern painters constitute movements instead of schools),[7] there is the unity imposed by at least some common interests and purposes. This emphasis on the generality of terms of criticism is the same point, developed in connection with Wittgenstein's arguments as analyzed in Chapter III, made earlier on the essential generality of reference and ostensive defining.

Any division of excerpts from critics into puristic, expressionistic, and naturalistic points of view or terms of attention will at times seem arbitrary.

This arbitrariness is most conspicuous in the division
between naturalism and expressionism with regard to
abstract paintings. Several of the examples from
Rosenberg could as well be classified under expressionism as naturalism. I would say only that the
line between expressionism and naturalism is indistinct, perhaps non-existent, where abstract works are
concerned, but I employ the classification because of
its usefulness with regard to more traditional critics.
I place in parentheses any introductory, transitional,
or concluding remarks I consider necessary to understand the passage from the critic. Further, I specify
in the parentheses the part of the passage which involves sensing. Finally, I use in the parentheses,
concepts such as describing or characterizing, and
these are defined later in Chapter VIII.

Purism

   Fry on Daumier's "Gar St. Lazare":

 If, however, having for the moment exhausted the
rich illustrational matter we return to the con-
templation of plastic relations we shall find, I
think that it is not possible to push them much
further. We find, no doubt, a generally coher-
ent and intelligible disposition of the volumes
in the space. The ample block made by the
colonel's figure creates the chief salience and
divides the space left to right satisfactorily--
or nearly so, for I find myself always wonder-
ing whether it should not be a little further
to the left for perfect balance; nor is it
after all quite big enough as volume to ful-
fill the function it has to perform. And this
failure in plastic completeness seems actually
due to Daumier's desire to bring out more clearly this particular dramatic incident.[9]

 (Fry describes the dominant plastic effect. He
visually analyzes the working of plastic qualities. He interprets, prior to the passage
given, the dramatic incident which caused Daumier to
lose his sense of plastic qualities. A verdict is given on the inadequacy of the plastic
qualities. Several claims about where the eye
is lead or drawn are made. Some inter-thing
plastic units are described. Plastic sensing
is involved in the consideration of subject
matter as masses, volumes, blocks and hori-
zontals, with the resultant lack of balance.)

Greenberg on Kandinsky:

(Greenberg argues that by 1920 Kandinsky was accepting the flatness and geometrical drawing of Synthetic Cubism without understanding the necessity in the relation of the two.)

Geometrical regularity, instead of preserving the tension and unity of the surface by echoing the regularity of its enclosing shape, became for Kandinsky a decorative manner that had little to do with pictorial structure. The surface remained, in effect, a mere receptacle, the painting itself an arbitrary agglomeration of shapes, spots and lines lacking even decorative coherence.[9]

(Greenberg describes and characterizes plastic effects, with strong value suggestions, leading to this verdict:)

We shall have to go on reckoning with him as a large phenomenon if not as a large artist.[10]

(Plastic sensing is involved in the claim that the geometrical regularity is merely decorative.)

Greenberg on Pollock:

By means of his interlaced trickles and spatters, Pollock created an oscillation between an emphatic surface--further specified by highlights of aluminum paint--and an illusion of indeterminate but somehow definitely shallow depth that reminds me of what Picasso and Braque arrived at thirty-odd years before, with the facet-planes of their Analytical Cubism.[11]

(Greenberg describes and explains the plastic effects. One senses the oscillating between flatness and shallow depth. We sense the plastic functioning.)

Naturalism

Ruskin on Turner's "Pass of Faido":

These trees Turner cuts away, and gives the rock a height of about a thousand feet; so as to imply more power and danger in the avalanche coming down the couloir.

Next, he raises, in a still greater degree,
all the moutains beyond, putting three or four
ranges instead of one, but uniting them into a
single massy bank at their base, which he makes
overhang the valley, and thus reduces it nearly
to such a chasm as that which he has just passed
through above, so as to unite the expression of
this ravine with that of the stony valley.[12]

(The whole passage is a sort of production explanation of reasons for changes Turner made on the scene. The reference "so as to imply more power and danger" is about intent to increase the sense of power and danger. Increasing the masses of the mountains which overhang the valley increases the sense of power of nature. Turner made some other changes to increase the sense of violence of the stream.)

    Rosenberg on Pollock and Hofmann:

Long Island or Woodstock underbrush enters an
abstraction by Pollock or Guston in a state
too primitive for definition except as substance in general. Similarly, the relation
between the gardens and sunlit walls of
Provincetown and the paintings of Hans
Hofmann must be established entirely by
tactile imagination; the last thing one
may expect to find is resemblance to details.[13]

(Rosenberg claims landscape can enter pure abstracts as "substance in general." He tells us that the abstracts are animated by underbrush, gardens and sunlit walls. These passages are supported by claims, made elsewhere in the essay, on how the act of painting taps the reservoir of the subconscious. Sensing is involved in the animation. It would be natural to say that Pollock gives a sense of underbrush or Hofmann of sunlit walls.)

<u>Expressionism</u>

    Baudelaire on Delacroix:

To complete this analysis, it only remains
for me to note one last quality in Delacroix--

but the most remarkable quality of all, and
that which makes him the true painter of the
nineteenth century; it is the unique and persistent melancholy with which all his works
are imbued, and which is revealed in his
choice of subject, in the expression of his
faces, in gesture and in style of colour.[14]

(Baudelaire gives a summary description of the
uniqueness of Delacroix, with an explanation
of what the melancholiness is due to. Sensing
is involved in the expression of faces, in the
gestures and in the color schemes.)

Gombrich on Leonardo's "Mona Lisa":

Everyone who has ever tried to draw or scribble
a face knows that what we call its expression
rests mainly in two features: the corners of
the mouth, and the corners of the eyes. Now
it is precisely these parts which Leonardo has
left deliberately indistinct, by letting them
merge into a soft shadow. That is why we are
never quite certain in what mood Mona Lisa is
really looking at us. Her expression always
seems just to elude us.[15]

(Gombrich explains the enigmatic expression
in terms of facial features. Sensing is involved in grasping the elusive facial expression.)

Several things need to be noted about these examples. In the first place, many of the examples involve what we might loosely call illusionistic qualities. In the Introduction and in Chapter II, it was
noted that "sense" can take such qualities. One of
the lines of the Müller-Lyer illusion gives a sense
of being longer than another. Even though sensing
was defined as containing a Perceptual Condition and
a Subtlety Condition, this only means there must be
cues to the impression, and only the cues are seen,
though the quality caused by the cue, the impression,
is sensed. These cues must be potentially sepcifi-
able, though we might not now be able to specify the
cues. The cues must be potentially specifiable in
order for sensing to be a perceptual act.[16]

Second, almost all the examples involve an explanation of some impression, as well as a description

of some impression. Fry explains the plastic imbalance in the Daumier. Baudelaire specifies the purported cues of melancholiness in Delacroix's works. Greenberg explains what causes the shallow space in Pollock. Gombrich explains what facial features give Mona Lisa such an elusive expression. Critics sometimes just synoptically describe impressions, but very often they explain the impression. Of course, cues cited in one explanation can themselves often be further explained, and there is no end to what can be in theory explained. Analogously, there are analytical styles of sensing, in which one looks at cues expecting some impression. Sometimes a more synoptic style of sensing is needed. There, of course, is no ultimate level for either explaining or sensing. Practically speaking, every act of sensing has some bottom level units of attention, but there is no reason someone else may not make these units themselves a gestalt to be explained or sensed analytically.

Lastly, to look ahead, one may note that ability and experience is presupposed if one is to evaluate the examples. One may learn to sense from the examples, but one has to have sensibility to evaluate the examples. If one does not have the ability to sense plastic qualities, one does not know whether the Daumier analyzed by Fry is imbalanced or not, nor what causes the purported imbalance. Without the ability to sense plastic qualities, one is not able to find Fry's analysis sound or unsound. The Greenberg comparison of the space of Pollock to those of Picasso and Braque presupposes experience with cubism, and presumably this experience with cubistic space presupposes ability to sense the subtleties of various kinds of picture space. Thus the Greenberg example seems to presuppose ability to sense space, as well as considerable exercise of this ability on examples of Analytical Cubism. One needs ability to sense as well as funded experience in sensing spatial qualities in puristic terms. Both ability and experience will be characterized below. Finally, the Clark example cited earlier seems to involve something different still. Specifying the elusive connotations of some group of paintings, in this case the very large group of Gothic Nudes, in terms of some ordinary objects which have similar connotations seems as much ability to imaginatively use language as it is any visual ability. But even here, Clark presumably sensed the Gothic Nude with clarity and distinction, for that is what happens to our sensing of them if we find his metaphor incisive. Rosenberg shows similar ability in describing Hofmann's "The Garden" as having become "a pavement of light through cliffs and jungles of fierce impasto."[17] Similarly in Hofmann's "Le Gilotin" the blobs of pigment are described as having become "clots of bituminized bananas."[18] Rosenberg shows the kind of imagination necessary to deal with the category crossings which occur in paintings. Pavements of light are very different from more usual beams of light, and bananas do not usually occur in clots or bituminized. Very different abilities and experience are presupposed if one is to find the examples sensitive, sound, perceptive, distorting, etc.

I have tried to show in this chapter how one may pedagogically take the terms of attention from critics in learning to sense. Taking the passages from critics pedagogically is very different from finding the passages from critics successful in various kinds of ways such as being sound, insightful, incisive, perceptive, etc. It is only after one has ability to sense and has employed that ability on a number of works that one can find the remarks sound, perceptive, etc. I have tried to show that learning to sense a painting is not different in kind from learning to see dim galaxies, learning to look at X rays, learning to look for the quary of the hunter, etc. All these visual abilities involve the redistribution of attention to the appropriate centers, groupings and aspects of objects of attention. Attention can be recentered by devices and techniques--eyeside, intermediate and object side--emphasized in the model of a visual act. Learning to sense is learning a perceptual ability, thus fulfilling the Perceptual Condition in the definition of sensing. When one has acquired the ability to sense, various forms of which are characterized below, one can explore the subtleties of paintings, thus satisfying the Subtlety Condition of sensing. Even occasional sensing, in contrast to the ability to sense, fulfills the Subtlety Condition.

ENDNOTES

[1] Baudelaire, p. 141.

[2] Fry, Transformations, pp. 16-18.

[3] Ruskin, IV, 24-25.

[4] Nelson Goodman, Languages of Art: An Approach to a Theory of Symbols (Indianapolis and New York: Bobbs-Merrill, 1968).

[5] Kenneth Clark, The Nude: A Study in Ideal Form (Garden City, N. Y.: Doubleday Anchor, 1956), p. 400.

[6] Wittgenstein, secs. 28-30.

[7] Renato Poggioli, The Theory of the Avant-Garde, trans. Gerald Fitzgerald (New York, Evanston, San Francisco, London: Harper and Row, 1971), pp. 17-20.

[8] Fry, Transformations, pp. 16-18.

[9] Clement Greenberg, Art and Culture: Critical Essays (Boston: Beacon Press, 1967), p. 113.

[10] Ibid.

[11] Ibid., p. 218.

[12] Ruskin, IV, 24-25.

[13] Rosenberg, The Anxious Object, p. 69.

[14] Baudelaire, p. 65.

[15] E. H. Gombrich, The Story of Art (London: Phaidon, 1966), p. 219.

[16] Roughly the cause of the Müller-Lyer illusion is something about the nature of the eye, ingrained scanning habits, knowledge of things like corners, etc. Even though no final explanation can now be given of a particular impression, any sensing that is genuinely visual must involve cues which are potentially, if not at present, specifiable. Although the model of a visual act deals with eyeside and intermediate (in-

cluding visual aids and verbal acts) matters in learning to sense, it is the painting, as a causally active field, which provides the uptake for sensing. A painting will provide a richer sort of sensing if it is looked at in the proper terms so its causally active field can work. Even though I think the form of explanation of sensing impressions in a painting is the same as the form of explanation of the Müller-Lyer illusion, paintings as causally active fields are very fragile and easily warped by the wrong terms of attention.

[17] Rosenberg, The Anxious Object, pp. 123-24.

[18] Ibid., p. 96.

CHAPTER V

ORIGINAL ELEMENTS OF ART

The most difficult sort of seeing is sensing original elements of art. There are such complex metaphysical problems here having to do with what we might call category flux or change that I will give only some hints about this most creative sort of seeing. Somewhat arbitrarily, I specify that "original" here means a painter appears to have made a decisive break with the history of art, and his new discoveries, techniques, procedures, conceptions, etc., are fruitful. I think we would not say a painter whose discoveries, techniques, and conceptions were a dead end was original. Many who speculate about the nature of originality think "original" means that the decisive break with tradition was only apparent, and on some deeper level there is continuity with the history of art. I need only the first emphasis, and we can generalize by saying originality is both a backward and forward looking concept. Further, it seems that a painter can have a style but not be original, but not conversely. Uniqueness of style is not the same as originality, though originality is a form of uniqueness. Differently put, originality must be specified in terms of elements of art: One always is original in some respect, but a painter can have elements of art and not be original (the elements of his art could be academic or simply not fruitful). A painter may be a great painter and not be original. It is just that originality seems to constitute a special problem for the emphasis on sensing in generalizable terms. A painting is a particular object, and our perception of it has a richness and fullness which exceeds the terms in which we describe it, and style and originality cover part of that je ne sais quoi we often feel the urge to express and the inability to express. I make these observations:

1) If I define original as fruitful, then we should learn to see in terms of the original work so that we can perceptively see the works which mined the original gems. Thus, even original works generate visual acts of some generality. It is also true that learning to see in certain terms, even when the terms were first derived from an articulation of originality, can become a habitual and rigid skill which prevents

us from seeing flexibly and creatively. A good way of describing the change from creative work to academic sterility is not only in terms of rigidity in the productive situation but also in terms of loss of creative seeing.

2) Dealing with original elements of art requires creative <u>verbal acts</u> as well as creative acts of seeing. Baudelaire said great criticism approached poetry. Whoever first said we should see Cézanne in terms of <u>planes</u> of color in space (a creative use of a reference aider) had poetic insight and expressiveness. Baudelaire's statement that Delacroix's line is never anything but "the intimate fusion of two colors, as in the rainbow"[1] is a stroke of expressive genius. Of course, we often later nominalize original discoveries we could describe only with metaphor, strange reference aiders, etc., as "painterly style" is, in a sense, a nominalization of Baudelaire's metaphor; and this point could be related, I believe, to what Wittgenstein said about there being no ultimate simples.[2]

3) There is a creative act <u>of vision</u> involved in describing original elements of <u>art</u>. What a critic says (with some exceptions not relevant here) is the criterion for how a painting appears or looks to him, and unless we want to say criticism is entirely a matter of an arbitrary projection into a painting of verbal functions, we have to say the critic <u>visually noticed</u> what he was able to verbally express. If we say remarks such as the above were <u>perceptive</u> and <u>insightful</u> with regard to the visual subtleties of a painting, we have to say that the critic, and now we, can <u>see</u> the painting in those terms. In distinguishing modes of vision from the verbal ways in which they are learned, I emphasized that we may consciously attend to something without being able to describe the object of attention. Visual exploring and noticing have an intentionality and uptake which is often unexpressed.

4) Not only does what we believe about criticism require that visual noticing be necessary for creative and incisive descriptions, but each of us, after very little experience, has been able to attend to some visual subtlety, felt it was fruitful and interesting, but felt an expressive block which a critic later relieved, and we said "that's exactly it." When we felt an expressive need due to our own visual noticing and exploring--that is the most satisfying sort of seeing

what the critic means. This most satisfying sort of communication at the level of the senses requires a creative act of vision, which we occasionally have, and a good critic has to have regularly.

5) Perceiving original elements of art is as much an art as a skill, but when the originality is *in* some visual subtlety (which often it is not), sensibility as perceptual refinement ability must be developed to sense the subtlety.

6) A most difficult question still is what relationship existent perceptual refinement abilities or ability to sense in certain terms have to seeing original work initially. Of course, if the original work exploits established terms of criticism in some interesting and different way, we at least have the ability to notice that sort of subtlety. If an entirely new mode of vision is called for, I am relatively certain we could not initially sense a work in that mode definitely and distinctly, even though we might find the work visually interesting and feel it is fruitful. I doubt that we can make very fine discrimination with regard to entirely new modes of vision, especially if the new modes do not have any counterpart in ordinary modes of vision. There may be a give and take between the verbal and visual analogous to the increases in the painter's sensibilities by production.

7) Original art requires originality or creativity on the part of the critic, and the forms this creativity may take are suggested in the analysis of resources of a visual act. The critic may be creative in devising new intermediate aids such as drawn overlays, in the inventive use of reference aiders, in suggesting new ways of using the eyes on the original art, and of course in creative verbal functions such as metaphors and attempts to describe and explain new and elusive qualities. My model of a visual act shows that we have considerable resources to learn to sense original art, and these resources include eye-side, intermediate and object-side aspects of visual acts.

ENDNOTES

[1] Baudelaire, p. 59.

[2] Wittgenstein, secs. 39-64.

CHAPTER VI

SENSING AS ABILITY: STAGES AND STYLES OF SENSING

Sensibilities evolve like beliefs, partially by being directed, partially by natural likes and dislikes, and partially by drift. Many things we have come to believe we did not will to believe. Some things we are even forced to believe against our will. There is an analogous drift in the development of our sensibilities. We have a vague desire to become cultured persons, and with regard to painting this desire may take the form of wanting to develop some form of sensibility; but despite this vague desire, our sensibility evolves partially by drift. I have isolated the deliberate part in terms of learning to sense as a visual act, and I try below to show that ability to sense can be in various states from bare appreciation to full sensibility to a kind of quality. I have developed a model of a visual act to idealize the intentional part in learning how to look at a painting. In effect, I sketched out what learning to sense various kinds of qualities (puristic, expressionistic or naturalistic) is like. In the model of learning to sense which I developed, I emphasized only the deliberate part having to do with vision, and the model is distorting in that sense.

My model of a visual act emphasizes an active development of sensibility. This emphasis, in a sense, rationalizes sensibility, in that it lessens the amount of drift, and in that it rationalizes our natural likes and dislikes by turning them into different sorts of likes and dislikes (the pleasures peculiar to various aesthetic positions). There is a stronger and a weaker sense of rationalizing. The stronger sense would be to make some activity a rational activity. This sense of rationalizing, of course, would destroy the nature of sensibility as a visual experience and ability. A weaker sense of rationality occurs when rational means, such as analytically learning how to sense, are employed to develop some ability which is not itself a form of rationality. (Aristotle is sometimes said to have confused these two senses of rationality.)[1] My model of a visual act rationalizes sensibility in this weaker and more legitimate sense. Learning of any sort is a rationalizing activity, and learning to sense is as well; hopefully, I have given some analytical detail to learning to sense.

When we analytically learn any ability, the lessons learned are appropriated by the relevant part of the perceptual motor self in any number of ways. Analogously, the model of a visual act gives analytical detail to how we learn to sense, and these lessons may be variously seated. We must distinguish the direction and <u>state</u> of our sensibility in terms of the ideal community of sophisticated viewers, critics, and paradigms at which we are aiming from the <u>style</u> of sensing. The diagram (Figure 5) shows an intermediate state of sensibility directed towards purism, and, of course, there are always possible changes in the state and direction of sensibility. The diagram also shows, in the solid arrows one is to imagine as on a plane at right angles to the page, styles of sensing. And the diagram introduces the idea of a first and second cutting edge with regard to terms of attention.

First and Second Cutting Edges

The first cutting edge is where critics are in the assimilation of some new terms of painting. Critics and very sophisticated viewers constitute the first cutting edge. Over time the best viewers of paintings make some progress in discovering the terms of viewing a certain painting, school of painting, period of painting, etc. It is impossible to discuss the nature of the first cutting edge without making extensive claims about the nature of art history and the role of criticism in relation to art history. Some sample disputes about the first cutting edge are these: What is the nature of progress, if any, in a school of art or within the work of a single painter? Views on this subject vary from Hegelian theses about a painter's internal development to nominalistic views that history is just one thing after another. Hegelians are fond of the idea that there is a natural life cycle in art. Within a style we see the birth, growth, maturation and decline of a style. This point of view can be applied within and between painters. A more nominalistic view would reject this sort of thesis. Critics usually do take an explicit stand on issues like these, for the role of criticism varies according to the way one conceives of progress or lack of it in the history of art. Subjects such as these cannot be discussed in any brief manner. Thus I will only discuss the second cutting edge--where a particular viewer is in his development.

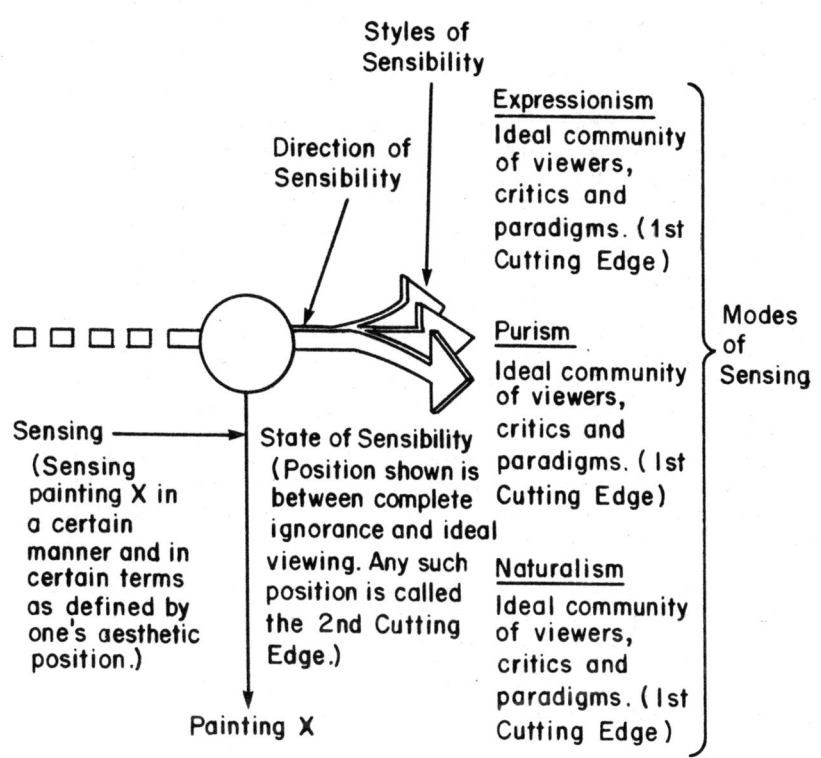

Figure 5

A discussion of the second cutting edge is simply a discussion of the styles and stages of sensibility. Thus, this whole chapter is a discussion of the second cutting edge.

Styles of Sensing: Factors in Ways the Model Can Be Seated

By "styles of sensing" I mean non-aesthetic or borderline aesthetic characteristics of the ability to sense--issues such as whether one should characterize sensing as a visual skill or as a more imaginative ability. For some purposes, issues such as these are more important than where one is in one's development along some line directed toward what one considers ideal viewers. But since I am limiting myself in this book to sensing in terms of aesthetic positions, the stages of sensing are more important than styles of sensing. One may suspect, incidentally, that answers to the question of what style of sensing one should acquire are related to one's view about the first cutting edge. If one believes originality is a key value of painting, one would want to develop a style of sensing which allowed rapid assimilation of new ways of painting. One would desire a style of sensing which was responsive to what I have called the category flux in painting images. Or by contrast, one may not be so much interested in assimilating the new as in sensing skillfully some school of painting or even some single painter.

I have occasionally spoken of practicing a visual act as though modes of sensing could be seated like habits, and, along the same lines, I have compared learning to see a painting to learning to see dim galaxies. Further, the model of a visual act, expecially the emphasis on eye techniques, makes it seem as though learning to see a painting can be a kind of skill, ultimately having the flow and smoothness of a skilled act. Attention is learning to see in certain terms. Attention of any complexity is like any learned skill. At first attention is clumsy, stiff, academic, and unresponsive, but later it can become smooth, and there will be a noticeable increase in perceptual refinement. Perceptual refinement is most literally specifiable in terms such as discrimination, acuity, and sensitivity. But even with regard to skilled acts like averted vision, such terms do not fully describe the skill. Averted vision requires motor skill in order to resist foveating the object of attention.

Further, it requires an ability to attend to a non-foveated region. Thus, even though averted vision increases sensitivity, sensitivity alone is not a sufficient description of the act. One-track discriminative abilities such as sensitivity, discrimination, or acuity are not sufficient specifications of any visual skill, especially not sufficient specifications of sensibility.

I think we do speak of the astronomer's observing abilities as visual skill, and certain forms of decontextualizing and emphasizing with regard to plastic qualities come close to being a skill. Thus we may conceive of a critic who is habituated to a certain mode of viewing or terms of viewing, and who is highly skilled in dealing with paintings for which that mode of viewing is adequate. At the same time, this critic, as the concept skill suggests, might not be able to apply his mode of seeing to original work which does not fit the terms of sensing he has learned and is proficient at. I believe that there are critics who are extremely perceptive on a very narrow band of work, sometimes only the work of a single painter, and the ability of these critics is best characterized as highly skilled viewing, which no doubt has a lot of clarity and depth for the limited range of work the mode fits, but which is not especially flexible. I think the model then can be seated as a skill, and the emphasis on eye techniques, focus of the eyes, and direction of attention certainly emphasizes the physical and physiological aspects of seeing. But it is also true that emphasis on the physical aspect of seeing is rather strained when applied to most critics.

At the other extreme, another kind of visual ability critics have might be characterized as <u>responsive noticing</u>. Isenberg's phrase "communication at the level of the senses" suggests to me a verbal function, such as a brilliant description, which achieves a tighter fit to the elusive quality of a painting or corpus of paintings. Rosenberg's description of the Hofmann ("bituminized bananas") and Clark's description of Gothic Nudes ("bulblike women and rootlike men") achieved for me a tighter fit, a fit which suggests a responsiveness to this particular painting or group of paintings instead of use of more ordinary and established terms of attention.[2] The visual ability part of sensibility thus is often more a form of responsive noticing than just seeing in certain terms.[3] Responsive noticing is the critic's counterpart of creativity in the painting. It means a responsiveness to the category flux creative images have.

One might question whether responsive <u>noticing</u> is consistent with my definition of sensing, since that definition includes a condition by which cues or variables can work without our being able to specify exactly what the cues are. My answer is that a painting's working is one thing, and <u>specifying</u> or <u>describing</u> the resultant quality or the cues which cause the quality is another; and that when a critic does succeed in describing a quality or cues, his verbal functions do show responsive noticing. Further, a critic can show responsive noticing in synoptic descriptions where some impression is described, but where no explaining cues are cited.

A <u>viewer</u> can have a counterpart of responsive noticing. I have argued that sensing as a visual mode is semi-independent of the verbal acts from which it is learned, and thus the sort of impression on which there is visual uptake when there are verbal acts can be grasped <u>without</u> verbal acts. When a critic gives a fresh articulation, as in Clark's description of Gothic Nudes, we do not want to say we had noticed the quality described, but we do assert that we had sensed Gothic Nudes in that way, but could not describe their elusive quality. Sensing is the viewer counterpart of the critic's responsive noticing. Sensibility which is independent from verbal acts means one has visually sensed some elusive quality or visually sensed how the rich context of cues and counter cues of the visual image is working. If sensing as a skill is one extreme of the visual ability in sensibility, sensing as responsive noticing is the other extreme. Responsive noticing seems to differ from visual skill in that responsive noticing is more closely connected to creative verbal acts, such as incisive descriptions, than are visual skills. One might be sensitive to plastic qualities, for example, and know how to describe a painting's working in those terms, but not have the sort of imagination involved in an incisive verbal description. Ability to express category flux is not the same as visual skill.

Ziff has observed that acts of visual exploring of paintings have different styles, and the style should be appropriate to the painting.

I survey a Tintoretto, while I scan an

H. Bosch. Thus I step back to look at the
Tintoretto, up to look at the Bosch. Different actions are involved. . . . Thus to
contemplate a painting is to perform one
act of aspection; to scan it is to perform
another; to study, observe, survey, inspect,
examine, scrutinize, etc., are still other
acts of aspection. There are about three
hundred words available here in English,
but that is not enough.[4]

My model of a visual act, and the ways it can be seated, explains different kinds and styles of visual exploring.

Another way of characterizing the difference between visual skill and responsive noticing is to relate them to the <u>different</u> <u>manners</u> in which experience with some style of painting is used. Most of us do not often achieve creative sensing, and in terms of experience this lack means we use our experience in a rather stilted and academic manner. A person whose sensibility is like a skill employs the same vocabulary habitually, and thus is sensitive to only a limited range of work. But there are ways of using experience with some aesthetic quality which are more creative and thus more suited to sensibility as a responsive noticing. To specify animation of the painting image by ordinary objects and allusion to objects and other paintings, we have to be sensitive to images of objects, combinations of objects, odd things, and ways objects are taken apart by painting acts in manners which are categorically bizarre in terms of our natural language and form of life. We may initially learn verbally how to look at a painting, but true sensing has some flexibility and independence from verbal instructions. This flexibility means that some critical verbal functions, such as describing elusive animation, are as much or more a matter of imagination than they are a matter of skilled ability with regard to attention in terms of the eye-side-object-side model of attention.

Imagination has traditionally meant a creative use of remembered material instead of a rigid use as in a skill. Imagination is involved when a critic's description achieves an incisive close fit, when he expresses the unexpressed, as suggested in Isenberg's phrase "communication at the level of the senses," whether the critic succeeds by entertaining many expressions, selecting just the right one, or whether he has the ability to just hit on the right one.[5]

Simply to answer the question "what am I seeing?" with regard to an abstract painting requires ability, and that ability is as much imagination as it is visual skill. With regard to traditional painting, to answer the question, "what is the nature of these ordinary objects?" requires the same sort of imagination. Questions about the nature of things in picture space are different questions from, "what kinds of objects are these?" To answer what kind of objects one is seeing, when they are clearly identifiable, does not involve sensing since such answers fail to satisfy the Subtlety Condition. Of course, I have suggested the concept of imagination as the creative counterpart, in the way experience is used, to sensibility as responsive noticing, and I emphasize here that specifying animation and many other verbal functions is as much a matter of imagination as visual skill. And, of course, imagination is not unrelated to creative verbal functions of critics. Merely to say, as Kenneth Clark does, that the Gothic Nude has the qualities of uprooted bulbs is a creative verbal feat, an incisive metaphor, which requires a rich imagination. In sum, I want to emphasize that the manner in which experience is employed is intimately connected to the style of the sensing, and that imagination expresses a way of using experience that is especially suited to responsive noticing.

Stages of Sensing: Direction and State of Sensibility

So far as the states of our sensibility go, I shall crudely divide them into three stages, the second and third being genuine sensing. The labels I shall give to the various states (which are indefinite in variety and style) of ability are: 1) Appreciation means that if we are verbally instructed on how and in what terms to look at a painting, we may then sense its impressions. Take the Fry analysis of the Daumier: Before we have any experience at all in sensing in terms of plastic qualities, we find that example baffling. We do not know whether the painting is imbalanced or not. Before we have ability to sense in certain terms, all we can really do is ask someone we trust on these matters questions such as: "Who is a good puristic critic?," "Who is a good critic of Daumier?", etc. At the stage of appreciation our sensibility to plastic qualities does not exist. 2) Sensing as Visual Exploring means visual exploration where we actually direct attention, as a

visual act, to proper terms and units of attention.
Here we are at the stage where we often sense certain
kinds of impressions without being specifically instructed. We visually experience impressions while
exploring the painting. We have learned to direct
attention to the visual intentional object. Our sensibility now has some autonomy from verbal and other
techniques through which we learned to sense impressions. 3) <u>Sensibility</u>, which goes beyond mere direction of attention, means ability to deal with the context and subtleties of that kind of impression. Of
course, sensing as sensibility does not mean we lack
the visual attention of the second stage. Our attention is more sophisticated in that it involves a
feeling for the relevant variables of some terms of
attention. Most aesthetic qualities involve many
variables, and sensibility, in contrast to sensing
as visual exploring, means a feeling for a weighting
of variables. Sensibility with regard to plastic
qualities, for example, would mean ability to sense
definite and distinct space of a certain nature, even
given all the cues and counterpoints in a rich painting context. Vaguely stated, sensibility means ability to deal responsively with the sort of impressions
paintings give. Of course, few of us except talented
critics achieve sensibility, except occasionally. A
more imaginative ability, in contrast to visual ability, is sometimes involved in sensing. These summarily stated distinctions need developing.

<u>Appreciation and Sensing As Visual Exploring</u>

The contrast between appreciation and sensing as
visual exploring can be developed succinctly in terms
of the previous analysis of visual acts. Suppose,
contrary to my arguments, that being an experienced
viewer meant one who simply <u>verbally</u> entertained an
active vocabulary of several different aesthetic positions to find the one fitting this painting. In the
case of the Fry example on Daumier, the viewer simply
alerts his verbal vocabulary to the terms of purism.
I repeatedly argued against this idea of experienced
viewing in emphasizing that even though attention may
be learned from verbal means, it is not necessarily
so learned, but even when so learned attention can become independent of the verbal instructions. I have
repeatedly emphasized that sensing is a <u>visual</u> exploring, and is not just saying to oneself (or having
someone else say) something and then sensing the
painting in that way. My model of a visual act

emphasizes the physical and even physiological aspects of learned visual acts. If we have really learned the terms of purism, we can visually explore paintings in those terms, and paintings actually <u>appear</u> or <u>give the impressions</u> purists and others discussed. Paintings can actually appear imbalanced if we know how to explore them in the terms of purism.

Sensing as an independent visual act of exploring, in certain terms, is not like occasional sensing, for sensing as exploring is at least in the right terms, units and centers of attention. One has some knowledge of the relevant cues and qualities, and attends to them, in contrast to simply having an elusive feeling of something. One does not yet have a feeling for the weighting of the variables, and thus sensing as visual exploring is different from sensing as full sensibility.

Sensing As Visual Exploring and Sensibility

The contrast between sensing as visual exploring and sensibility is more difficult to see than the contrast of appreciation and sensibility as visual exploring, for the kind of wisdom involved in sensibility is hard to characterize, and I shall introduce the idea of <u>experience with</u> terms of attention to try to characterize this wisdom. Deliberate and conscious recall, especially of verbal instructions, does not cover some of the most important aspects of our accumulated knowledge gathered from repeated encounters with something. Many things we know, especially things we know how to do, though we have learned and not forgotten them, seem not to be exactly memories. When a skilled artisan practices his craft with his equipment and tools, he does not exactly remember how to do what he does. He is skilled in his craft, and sometimes past problems may be remembered as warnings or positive pedagogy, but the basic part of the skill that comes to operate in the context of its usual employment is more like the sort of knowing and wisdom we call experience with something. Verbal lessons may have been once important in learning the skills, and remembering the lessons may have been once important, but for a skilled craftsman that sort of thing is now relegated to his trained hand. If we call all the things a craftsman has to deal with "variables," we can characterize this wisdom as the accumulation of a suitable set of weighted variables.

The idea of experience with something I think is

an especially suitable characterization of some kinds
of sensibility mentioned. A person who has a good
sense of character has had experience with all the
variables which reveal character, and he knows which
of those variables are more important or more weighted
than others. Analogously, a person with a good sense
of distance knows the variables which are signs of
distance, and he knows which of the variables is the
most important. I think the accumulation of an adequate set of weighted variables, through experience
with some sort of object, is in fact what we mean when
we attribute a sense of something to a person.

    However, there is a significant problem in whether
<u>ordinary</u> abilities to sense, such as having a sense of
character or a sense of distance, are transferable to
painting, and thus whether one can characterize <u>sensing
in terms of some aesthetic position</u> as a matter of accumulation of a proper set of weighted variables. There
really are two questions here: Whether the <u>particular
weighting</u> of variables in <u>ordinary</u> sensing carries over
to their <u>painting</u> analogue? And, whether <u>some</u> weighted
set of perceptual variables operates in a painting context, and thus whether we can say sensing paintings is
a visual <u>ability</u>, though not the ordinary counterpart
of that ability? I shall answer no to the first question and yes to the second. If the second answer
works, sensing is an ability gotten from experience
with, say, plastic qualities, an experience which has
lead to the accumulation of an adequate set of weighted
variables. Sensing as an ability, or full sensibility,
in contrast to sensing as visual exploring, will be defined in terms of a feeling for the relevant variables.

    The reason the <u>particular</u> weighting of variables
in ordinary forms of sensing does not carry over to
painting is fairly easy to see. Whole <u>dimensions</u> of
information about character, for example, available
to the ordinary judge of character, are unavailable
in paintings. The sound and cadence of speech, in
combination with gestures we can see, may be essential to judging, say, when someone is lying in ordinary life. A liability of caricature is that such
whole dimensions are not available. Not even all
<u>visual</u> information is available in caricature. If
we consider special sensibles of vision, there are
liabilities in caricature. We can visually perceive
a person's behavior <u>over time</u>. The caricature is a
fixed image. Of course, caricature has assets too.

We can contemplate and return to the fixed image in a way we could not with an actual person there staring back at us. More importantly, the caricaturist can orchestrate many elements to make character clearer in caricature than in ordinary life. He can clear away details, place the figures in striking places and poses, use light to draw attention, use color to draw attention, etc. Features of faces and postures are not so highlighted in ordinary life. Many elements other than those in ordinary life are used to draw attention to character. The ordinary judge of character has to sort out the relevant facial and postural and other physiognomic features. The caricaturist can exaggerate all these and he can use light and line to draw attention. Light and line are entirely new kinds of attention attractors available in caricature but not in life. Both the assets and the liabilities mean there has to be some radical reweighting of the relevant variables when one directs attention to characters in caricatures. A good judge of character in ordinary life will not necessarily be the best judge of character in caricature.

Analogous arguments can be given about picture space, for example. The whole dimension of tactile information is not available in picture space. Further, special visual sensible cues are not all available. Change of visual overlap with motion is a very important cue to space perception in ordinary life, and it is completely unavailable in paintings. Visual texture can be exaggerated to increase a sense of space. Athletes and hunters are not the best judges of picture space, though they are very experienced in ordinary spatial judgments.

The answer to the second question, whether it is reasonable to think there is some set of weighted variables relative to sensing paintings, though not the ordinary set, requires a digression into theory of vision. Specifically, I must comment further on the idea of weighted variables. Polemics in psychology, in theories of vision, are conducted, as one might expect from polemics, as though the variables were in some sort of hierarchy. Then, there are proponents of various favored variables at the top of the hierarchy, as there are proponents of texture as the most important cue to space versus the proponents of change of overlap as the most important cue to space. And there are, as admitted by all, equal weight redundancies. Both texture and change of overlap with motion are cues to space whether they are hierarchically ordered variables or equally weighted redundant variables. A reasonable guess about the future of theories of vision is that there will turn out to be some weighting of variables as well as some equal weighted variables, and they may vary from context to context.

Presumably when whole dimensions of information bearing sensory information are left out, as speech in caricature or cues while moving in space perception, there has to be a radical reshuffling of the variables. This reshuffling might destroy hierarchies, create new hierarchies, reduce some hierarchy to equal weighted variables, cause some equal weighted variables now to be hierarchically structured, etc. Some radical changes may be expected since some purely visual information is not given in the fixed image of a painting. Omission of the very important cue of change of overlap with motion surely affects hierarchically ordered variables and equal weighted variables relevant to depth perception. The upshot of this change is that sensitive, natural or suitable terms of viewing paintings are not necessarily the same as those in ordinary life. However, even ordinary forms of sensing, such as having good judgment about distance, show considerable flexibility in the handling of variables, both equal weighted variables and hierarchically ordered variables. Thus a reasonable conjecture about admittedly distant discoveries about vision seems to me to be this: Given some ordinary viewer with weighted variables in whatever hierarchies there are and with whatever equal weight redundancies there are, these will assume certain definite form given the assets and liabilities of paintings, and that a new "natural" form of weighted variables or redundant variables will result. This reasoning is a speculative argument, but it seems to me to be a reasonable argument given what is now known about vision.

There is a very different sort of argument from the <u>meaning</u> of sensing. Sensing is a perceptual mode (The Perceptual Condition). Since sensing also includes impressions, and these have to be caused by the painting as a visual field, I think we are <u>claiming</u>

some definite impression (due to equal weighted variables or hierarchically ordered variables) when we say a painting gives a sense of imbalance, etc. If sensing is distinct from imagining as, the painting has to determine the impression we claim to sense. The ordinary meaning of sensing certainly does not extend to the explanation of some impression in terms of equal weight or hierarchically ordered variables, but if sensing a painting really is a mode of perception, we would expect some causal explanation, in terms of the nature of the eye, of definite impressions. If we really sense impressions in paintings, the explanations of what causes those impressions will not differ in kind from the explanation of the Müller-Lyer illusion. Thus a claim that a painting gives a sense of imbalance, etc., does mean that the painting does give this impression. Of course, one might not be able to sustain this particular claim.

One might well admit that ordinary "prognostic" perception, to use Gombrich's expression, is the accumulation, through experience, of an adequate set of weighted variables. Through correction and reinforcement of successes, one might learn to center his attention more keenly on cues in a thing's looks as to how the thing really is. But there is a special problem, already indicated, in questions about how a thing really looks when this is not a question about how the thing really is. One might raise the criticism that, unlike ordinary prognostic perception, sensing an impression allows no correction and reinforcement, and thus no sense of accumulating an adequate set of weighted variables for some kind of quality. I think Tormey has adequately answered this question in his argument that discussions in criticism are more like mutual corroboration than they are like the more rigorous confirmation of the physical sciences.[6] Thus I would say that the correction and reinforcement of sensing an impression of paintings comes from dialogue with some critical community. One's unarticulated sensings are sometimes expressed by a critic, and often what one thought one had sensed, one will decide he did not sense. I think this is full-fledged correction and reinforcement, and thus I see no problem in the idea of accumulating an adequate set of weighted variables for sensing impressions of paintings. Further, it is important to emphasize that even in describing ordinary impressions we have no corroboration except the statements of others. We know how the Müller-Lyer illusion really appears to others because of what they tell us. Finally, the idea of a painting as a causal field, as analyzed in the last chapter, provides a distinction between how a painting really looks or appears versus imagining it a certain way. There a theoretical distinction is drawn between really appears or really gives an impression and imagining an impression.

In summary, I conclude that these speculative extensions of theory of vision mean we can think of sensibility as analogous to ordinary visual abilities. Both sensing a painting's impressions and ordinary forms of sensibility can be characterized as the accumulation of a feeling for the variables in some perceptual context. I thus differentiate sensing as visual exploring from sensing as sensibility in terms of experience with the terms of some aesthetic position. This last distinction completes the analysis of the stages and styles in which the model of a visual act can be ingrained in the eye-mind.

ENDNOTES

[1] W. F. R. Hardie, "The Final Good in Aristotle's Ethics," Philosophy, 40 (1965), pp. 277-95.

[2] Both phrases are quoted in context above. Rosenberg, The Anxious Object, p. 124. Clark, p. 400.

[3] See Aschenbrenner's definition of sensibility as "creative receptivity." Karl Aschenbrenner, The Concepts of Criticism (Dordrecht and Boston: Reidel, 1974), p. 72. See also the remarks above on the viewer's counterpart of the critic's verbal creativity.

[4] Ziff in Margolis, ed., Philosophy Looks at the Arts, p. 175.

[5] There are, of course, constructive, as well as articulative, senses of imagination, as Michaelangelo and Rembrandt would be said to have great imagination in conceiving their subjects.

[6] See Tormey's argument that we can corroborate, but not confirm, critical judgments. Alan Tormey, "Critical Judgments," Theoria, 39 (1973), pp. 35-49.

CHAPTER VII

THE ROLES OF PAINTINGS IN DEVELOPING SENSIBILITY

Models, Defining Examples and Paintings with Other Statuses

The problem, in the previous chapter, about the new weighting of variables in viewing painting means, of course, that paintings are the best embodiments of painting qualities even when these qualities have ordinary analogues, as picture space has analogues in ordinary space and character in caricature has analogues in ordinary character traits. Paintings will embody whatever new hierarchies of variables are created, whatever old ones destroyed, whatever equally weighted variables now become hierarchically ordered, and whatever equal weighted variables are created or left by the transfer from ordinary life to paintings. Thus, we can expect paintings to play a prominent role in the accumulation of the kind of wisdom meant by experience with picture space, etc.

Since paintings are the best embodiments of painting impressions such as picture space, we can expect paintings to play an important role in learning to sense. It is by repeated sensing of paintings that one develops the sort of wisdom suggested by claims such as "I have had a good deal of experience with plastic qualities." Paintings have many statuses for critics and viewers. Models have the highest status so far as aesthetic values go. Ruskin is very clear that Turner is his main model, and Baudelaire that Delacroix is his. Fry is less committed to a single model, but he obviously thinks highly of Cézanne and African sculpture. Rosenberg gives high placement to some of the Action Painters. Models are in fact part of the definition of the ideal experience of viewing for any critic. In addition, a critic will specify the faculties, abilities, knowledge and experience which constitute an ideal viewer. Since models are the embodiment of the best, in a value sense, of some aesthetic quality, one who is learning to sense would do well to learn the critic's terms and kinds of attention in relation to the critic's models. One should practice the resources of the visual act, using any intermediate aids the critic has given, on the critic's models. In a real sense, Fry means by plastic qualities the impression given by Cézanne and

Negro Sculpture. The verbal intentional object, for Fry, of the term "plastic" is Cézanne's paintings, Negro Sculpture and other works. Likewise, Baudelaire and Ruskin mean by imagination the works of Delacroix or Turner respectively.[1] To put it another way, it is paintings which exhibit puristic qualities such as imbalance in picture space or expressionistic qualities such as the meaning of masses in relation to human figures or naturalistic qualities such as insight into nature. These qualities are defined by paintings and not by their ordinary analogues. In summary, in learning to sense a kind of quality, one should especially practice discounting certain features and emphasizing others in the critic's models.

A very different status paintings can have in critics is defining examples. Defining examples are usually set up to enable the critic to characterize those paintings he feels it necessary to classify. Baudelaire defines three kind of draughtsman--the exact or silly, the physiognomic and the imaginative.[2] Delacroix is an example of the imaginative, as one might expect, but the other classes have a different status from models, and he uses the physiognomic as a label for Ingres' kind of draughtsmanship. But the point of defining examples in relation to sensing is that the defining examples introduce some differentiation into a certain element of art, in this case drawing. Critics not only specify some paintings as being the highest, as in say plastic qualities, but subdivide elements of art into different types. In learning to sense plastic qualities, one learns some finer discrimination. Greenberg, in the example above where he compares Pollock's space to that of the Analytical Cubism of Picasso and Braque, presupposes ability to sense in terms of such subtleties. One might need to learn to sense, for example, the difference between the spaces of Analytical Cubism and Cézanne, and both kinds of space need to be differentiated from but related to the spaces of the Abstract Expressionists. Thus one should practice the critic's basic terms of criticism on defining examples of those terms. This kind of practice will give an important part of experience with the terms of criticism for that critic.

In Chapter III, I argued that in a context of linguistic activities such as referring, we have many resources to direct the hearer's or reader's attention to the appropriate thing or aspect of the thing meant. The act of visual attention in a context of these linguistic activities is often completed by noticing the relevant object or aspect of some object, and in such cases we literally see what someone means. The actual visual uptake in the noticing completes the purpose of directing attention. Analogously, critics use all the resources suggested in my model of a visual act in order to develop sophisticated attention in the viewer, and ideally the models and defining examples provide the uptake in noticing which completes the act of attention, and we see what the critic means by some term like plastic qualities. Since paintings are very complex contexts, we are often not sure what a critic means. We may even be unsure about what the basic terms of his criticism mean, as there is considerable uncertainty in my mind about what Bell means by "significant form." But what is sure is that Bell means some quality in the models and defining examples he specifies. The meaning of the terms of criticism, especially given the problem analyzed in the carry over of ordinary sensibilities to painting, is always some painting or group of paintings. Thus follows the fundamental importance of learning the critic's mode of attention with regard to his models and defining examples. Hopefully, one will be able to actually see or notice what the critic means.

Most painters discussed by a critic have neither the status of a model nor defining example, and sometimes we finally come to see what a critic means by his basic terms through his analysis of some painting or painter other than the critic's models and defining examples. But whenever this indirection occurs, we should look again at the critic's models and defining examples, for these purportedly give the most direct specification of what the critic means by some term like plastic quality. Thus we should practice, in trying to learn to sense in certain terms, discounting and emphasizing as visual acts on the critic's models, defining examples and other paintings described, characterized, interpreted or explained.

Even though I have compared the visual ability of learning to sense a painting in certain terms to other visual abilities such as those of astronomers or readers of X rays, an important distinction now must be drawn. Models and defining examples mean that the terms of any critic are importantly shaped by <u>traditions of viewing</u>. These traditions contain definitions of visual styles such as the style of late baroque painting. We learn to see what a critic means by discounting and emphasizing visually with regard to his tradition of painting, and of course paintings understood as defining examples of aesthetic position are just this idea. More importantly, the tradition contains, as the idea of models suggests, works whose viewing is <u>valuable</u>. The point of learning to sense in certain terms is ultimately to be able to have the kind of enjoyment relevant to the aesthetic position chosen. The existence of a tradition containing defining examples and models, then, seems to me a significant difference between sensibility as a visual ability and other visual abilities. (However, in amateur astronomy, there are in a sense traditions, as in the descriptions of celestial objects by famous astronomers.)

It does not follow, of course, that just because one has had exposure to the critic's models and defining examples, in the terms of attention as specified by that critic, that one has automatically achieved the kind of wisdom involved in claims such as "I have considerable experience with plastic qualities in paintings." One can repeatedly encounter something without learning anything about it, and claims to have experience with something include the claim that one accumulated some wisdom or feeling for the thing in question. Thus I do not claim that the practice of my model of a visual act, as given specificity by the critic's models and defining examples, will automatically give one the proper set of weighted and equal weight variables necessary for sensibility of some kind. However, the concept of experience with some terms of attention understood as a feeling for hierarchies of variables and as a feeling for equal weight variables is a good characterization of the ability to sense. Experience with models, defining examples, and other paintings, in the suitable terms of attention, gives one a feeling for the relevant variables. Sensibility as ability differs from sensing as visual exploring in having this feeling for the relevant variables.

These remarks should make it clear that the characterization of experience with terms of attention is flexible enough to include differences in styles of ability, differences which vary from skills to responsive noticing. Thus sensibility to some kind of quality, a feeling for the weighting of these kinds of variables, can vary from skill to responsive noticing. Experience with terms of attention can also be used in various manners.

Funded Experience

Critics not only presuppose experience with sensing a certain kind of quality, as evaluation of Fry's analysis of Daumier presupposes experience in sensing plastic qualities, but experience of certain grouping of works, the grouping being implicit in the way the critic refers to paintings. Sometimes the grouping is a painter's corpus of works, as above where Baudelaire tries to express the elusive quality of Delacroix's work. Sometimes the grouping is a whole school, sometimes only a single painting is meant. These kinds of groupings are a different kind of classification than the kind emphasized in the analysis of terms of a critic, and thus a different classification is needed here. I shall call this sort of grouping presupposed in examples from critics funded experience of a specified class of works. Further, not only must we consider the kind of grouping in the critic's reference, but the kind of grouping, accidental or intentional, in which the viewer's experience has been accumulated. A viewer may look at any show that comes to a certain gallery. He may go to certain museums. He may seek out the work of a single painter. All these are different sorts of groupings, and give a different body of funded experience for the critic to articulate. Greenberg in comparing Pollock to the Analytical Cubism of Picasso and Braque is presupposing some funded experience in viewing Picasso, Braque and Pollock, as well as presupposing experience with sensing in terms of plastic qualities. Most of the examples from the critics in Chapter IV require ability and funded experience. Stated differently, we develop ability to sense in certain terms, have experience with those terms, exercise this ability on some grouping of works, and accumulate a body of funded experience that needs articulating. There are these two senses of experience, one an ability, the other the result of exercising that ability, which we need to mention. One might also suspect, as seems to be the case, that the kind of grouping both critics and viewers use has something to do with their views of the first cutting edge. Theories or views about the nature of art history will often influence the way one organizes his experience with paintings.

There is a different sense of funded experience relevant to naturalisms and expressionisms, namely a funded experience of life. Both naturalists and expressionists claim paintings articulate unexpressed experience. Ruskin claimed Turner captured the soul of the scene in "Reitz near Samur," and Ruskin generalized from many examples where Turner purportedly captured the soul of some landscape to general truths about experience and nature. Rosenberg even claimed abstract works could express nature. One can sense the sunlit walls of Provincetown in Hofmann, and the underbrush of Long Island in Pollock. Earlier, I discussed what I called the problem of carry over of ordinary insight to painting. We might call the expression of funded experience of life in art the problem of carry back, and this sort of articulation of experience is certainly essential to expressionisms and naturalisms.

Both the idea of experience with terms of attention and the idea funded experience of a group of paintings can be related to the idea of a visual act. In fact there seems to be a sort of feedback from experience to the act of attention. Ulric Neisser argues in Cognition and Reality that funded experience leads to further refinement of attention, which leads to further enriching of funded experience, which leads to further refinement of attention, etc.[3] Thus the progress from appreciation, to sensing as visual exploring to full sensibility is understandable in terms of experience with certain terms and funded experience. Both experience with certain terms and funded experience refine and are refined by an increasingly sophisticated mode of attention.

The concept of experience is of course a favorite concept of American Pragmatists such as Peirce and Dewey, and the origin of the idea of a sort of wisdom accumulated by doing is found at least as early as Aristotle (empires). Practical activities force us to refine relevant modes of perception. The model of a visual act simply emphasizes ways we can analytically refine attention to paintings. Since we do not handle paintings the way we handle objects in practical activities, development of aesthetic sensibilities must be purely visual. A condition of sensing is the Selective Knowledge condition, and the concept of experience has the connotations that something is learned by repeated encounters with that sort of thing in contrast to some special sort of learning such as learning symbolism of important historical, mythological or religious personages and events. Thus the accumulation of experience is the way one would expect sensing as an ability to be characterized, given the Selective Knowledge Condition. Further, we often think of forms of sensing, for example, having a good sense of character, as being part of that vague body of wisdom we call common sense. A person with a wide range of sensibilities is just a person with common sense. And the idea of experience, of course, fits very well with the idea of common sense. Experience with some terms of attention and funded experience of some grouping of works thus share with the ordinary concept experience the meaning of wisdom accumulated by repeated encounter and interaction with something.

At first it may seem odd to relate the impressions a painting gives us to abilities, experience with terms of attention and funded experience. Having good judgment is one thing, and how a painting appears is another. But I think it is not odd to relate abilities to impressions. Obvious impressions, such as the impression of a longer line given by the Müller-Lyer illusion or the effect of increased intensity of adjoining complementary colors, require no ability to sense, but elusive and subtle impressions of paintings do require ability to sense. We recall Austin's distinction between definite impressions we cannot describe and indefinite, shifting, ambiguous, and vague impressions we cannot describe.[4] The way we, as beginners, sense a painting is with vague and indefinite impressions. The impressions paintings give, like our dream image, are fragile tissues in which we are uncertain whether questions we ask or are asked are shaping or articulating the image. But with experience and developed abilities the impressions stabilize, and we are more certain what impressions a painting gives us, and I am calling this stabilizing core of perceptual abilities "sensibilities."

A look ahead suggests another way of summarizing the results of the last two chapters: A way of summarizing the plurality of ways the model may be seated as a visual ability is to emphasize that <u>visual</u> abilities we attribute to critics are inferences from repeated excellence in some <u>verbal functions</u> of critics; and thus the abilities learned can be expected to have the same plurality and richness as excellence in various verbal functions of critics. Visual abilities of critics, like all other abilities, are inferred from repeated excellent performances. Abilities have this similarity to character traits. Since the visual ability is learned from a variety of verbal acts, the nature of abilities can be indefinitely varied, and I characterized only some major styles. Another way of making these same points is to emphasize that the viewer usually learns to sense from verbal functions of critics, and thus the viewer's developed sensibility will have some of the style of the verbal functions to which he is partial. This sort of plurality in styles of sensing will be emphasized further in the next chapter in analyzing the rich range of expressions of perlocutionary force and in analyzing factors affecting perlocutionary force of speech acts.

ENDNOTES

[1] Of course, only part of what Baudelaire and Ruskin mean by imagination do I mean by sensing, though I did show that for both of them imagination is a perceptive faculty. Fry does direct us to employ only our sensibility on paintings, and Rosenberg's tactile imagination is related to what I mean by sensing.

[2] Baudelaire, p. 59.

[3] Ulric Neisser, <u>Cognition and Reality: Principles and Implications of Cognitive Psychology</u> (San Francisco: W. H. Freeman and Company, 1976). See especially pp. 20-24; 110-13.

[4] Austin, pp. 60-61.

CHAPTER VIII

SOME EPISTEMOLOGICAL ISSUES

The first epistemological implication of my theory of sensing is that sensing is presupposed in various kinds of successes of various critical verbal acts such as describing, interpreting, characterizing and explaining impressions of paintings. Thus we must see how successful speech acts are related to sensing. A second epistemological implication is that one can have self-knowledge of the state, direction and style of one's sensibility, and this self-knowledge affects the way one evlauates verbal acts of critics. A third, related epistemological implication, involves arguments against a relativistic view of critical judgments. The major division in this chapter corresponds to these three epistemological implications of the theory of sensing.

Intended and Achieved Perlocutionary Force

Austin used the term "perlocutionary force" to mean the aspect of speech acts having to do with the effect of some speech act on the hearer. A hearer might be warned by the remark "the bull is coming." Hearers can be warned, intimidated, convinced, skeptical, persuaded, etc. A speaker does not have full control over the perlocutionary aspect of speech acts, for the hearer's knowledge, opinions, beliefs about the speaker, ability to follow arguments, native credulity, etc., all affect the perlocutionary force achieved. Since speakers do not have full control over perlocutionary force, we do not use perlocutionary force verbs in the first person present tense. We can say "I promise" for it is within our power to commit ourselves to doing something, but it is not in our power to succeed in warning someone or convincing someone, and thus the uselessness of "I convince you that."[1] Even though we cannot control perlocutionary force achieved, we do intend to have certain effects on the hearer in speaking. Thus we can discuss both critic's intent to achieve certain perlocutionary forces such as being witty, sound in their analyses, incisive in their descriptions, etc.; and we can discuss what effect the viewer's sensibility and knowledge have on the critic's success. Also one final bit of technical terminology will be helpful: Philosophers speak of appraisers of linguistic acts such as describing or characterizing, and appraisers are such concepts as true, insightful, perceptive, sound, etc. Appraisers describe various perlocutionary forces intended and sometimes achieved. They are words used to label various kinds of successes and failures of functions of language such as descriptions, characterizations, interpretations or explanations. Another way of discussing the two sides of the perlocutionary aspect of linguistic acts, the speaker's side and the hearer's side, is in terms of intended and achieved appraisers.

Intended Perlocutionary Force

The concept of the basic terms of a critic's position has already been discussed, and the model of sensing was developed to explain learning to see in certain terms such as puristic, expressionistic or naturalistic. Critics, however, do not just employ terms, but employ the terms of their criticism in linguistic acts such as describing, interpreting, characterizing and explaining, and these different linguistic acts affect both the style of criticism and the style of sensing. Different linguistic acts are a constitutive part of intended perlocutionary force. Thus some brief characterization of these very vague concepts is necessary.[2] I also emphasize that certain critics rarely practice some of the functions listed. For example, Ruskin and Baudelaire rarely give the sort of visual explanations, analyses of plastic qualities, that is typical of Fry's <u>Transformations</u>. Fry, on the other hand, rarely does the sort of interpretation of meaning of a scene which is characteristic of Ruskin. A very important thing to note about the style of a critic is his partiality to or avoidance of certain functions practiced by other critics.

"Interpreting" or "interpret" can mean the whole aspect of criticism which is primarily non-evaluative, in the sense of explaining or understanding or appreciating a work. Here I use it in the more specific ordinary sense dealing with the meaning of a painting, and by "meaning" I shall mean a discussion of a painting in what we might broadly characterize as psychological terms. A paradigm of interpretation in this sense is the lengthy passages in Diderot which tell us what the various characters in a painting are like, what they are thinking and feeling, what the meaning of the dramatic incident in the painting is, etc.[3] Interpretation in a less moralistic sense can mean any treatment of a painting with human subjects in terms of their characters, natures, meanings, interactions in some incident, and the emotive tones of the whole. But even though paradigms of interpretations are of paintings with human subjects, this sort of broadly psychological term can be extended to non-human subjects, and even to pure abstracts. One could interpret a landscape or still life in describing its mood or emotive tone. Expressionists, as one might infer, are fond of interpreting.

"Characterize" is related to character, the habits of a moral quality that one repeatedly shows. Characterization by critics is thus naturally taken to mean the visual habits (analogues of character traits) a painter has which make up his visual style, and thus characterizing a painter consists in placing him in the history of styles. If one said Pollock's space was primarily the space of late Cubism, that is a characterization. If one says, as Baudelaire does, that Corot is more of a harmonist than a colorist, that is characterizing.[4] The classifications a critic has set up, including his defining examples, operate heavily in his characterizations. "I would characterize Cezanne as ____" is naturally used to classify or characterize Cézanne. Visually structuring or organizing a painting in terms of previous styles is a very important function of critics, and this kind of structuring can obviously be related to the new centers of attention, grouping of objects and structuring emphasized by my model of a visual act.

Descriptions overlap characterizations. "I would describe Pollock as having Cubistic space" seems as natural as "I would characterize Pollock as having Cubistic space." But there are many descriptions which are not characterizations. Descriptions, poetic or mundane, tell us what one sees in a painting or group of paintings with no attempt to place that painting or group of paintings in relation to other paintings. Descriptions do not take seasoned judgment, though they may require other abilities, as in poetic descriptions. Baudelaire achieved an expressive accomplishment when he described Delacroix's line as nothing but the intimate fusion of two colors as in a rainbow. Baudelaire even "attempted to express these subtle sensations" of Delacroix in his poetry.[5] When Clark describes the elusive tone of Gothic Nudes, as contrasted with Renaissance nudes, in terms of uprooted bulbs, we again feel some elusive quality has been rescued from the unexpressed. Expressing some elusive quality or tone is a demanding form of description. More mundane forms of descriptions are simply a recounting in words of the subjects in a painting, what they seem to be doing, what colors they are, whether the painting is a landscape, what the basic structure of the picture is, the forms in the picture, the placement of color areas, etc. Before prints were widely available, critics practiced extensively this word picture form of description.

"Explain" is a very broad function, meaning a critic's answer to a why question in terms of reasons or causes. Critics often give causal explanations of a painter's style in terms of the painter's environment, as Ruskin explains Turner's pessimistic and tragic view as due to Turner's youth in London.[6] One can give an explanation in terms of the painters a painter has studied . Intention explanations give the painter's purpose or reason for doing something. A most important kind of explanation in terms of learning to sense is the visual explanation. Critics often try to determine the visual cause or cues of some effect in a painting, as, for example, the cause of the imbalance of a composition or the luminosity of a color scheme. Fry's whole book *Transformations* is a set of visual explanations of how paintings, and other art works, function in a plastic sense. Visual explanations often border on optical, psychological and even physiological questions.

Reasons and conclusions are not the same sort of distinction as those above, for they refer to the structure and place various functions occupy in an argument and are not independent functions, as are functions like describing. Specifically, a characterization could be a conclusion from any number of linguistic acts such as visual explanations, interpretations, or descriptions. The nature of the conclusion and the nature of the reasons differ. Verdicts, rankings, characterizations, or value classing (the status of being a genius versus the status of being a minor master, for example) are different sorts of conclusions. Fry, for example, after giving a visual explanation of a painting in terms of plastic quality, often reaches some value-loaded conclusion, having the nature of a characterization, about the painting. Other more literary types of critics, such as Ruskin and Baudelaire, frequently reach a value-laden characterization after descriptions of various sorts. Baudelaire, after interpreting several of Delacroix's paintings, reaches the summary description that one of his most pervasive qualities is a unique and persistent melancholy.[7] Just as there are different kinds of reasons, there are kinds of conclusions--verdicts, condemnations, characterizations, rankings of all sorts, praise with all levels of tone, etc. Reasons and conclusions then do not signify independent sorts of functions, but rather indicate the place various functions come in an argument, some functions serving as reasons for other functions as conclusions. Analogous remarks are true of the widely practiced activity of comparing painters. Critics compare painters and paintings by describing, characterizing, explaining or interpreting one or both painters or paintings.

These linguistic functions must now be understood in terms of the specialization placed on them by my definition of sensing. Explanations of influences on a painter, excluding influences of other paintings, will be rarer, since sensing as I define it emphasizes, as does new criticism of literature, the work itself. Intention explanations will be in terms of ways the painter intended to exploit vision, often in the form of an explanation in terms of some known correlation, such as Cézanne attempting to create space by colored planes alone. Only knowledge gained from a background of visual normalcy can enter the explicans, given the Selective Knowledge Condition. Interpretation done within the limits of sensing will have to direct attention to features of expression, in both an intra-and inter-thing sense, which are keys to subtleties of expression. Other matters relevant to interpretation, such as the identity of some mythological or religious personage, do not fall within the definition of sensing. Characterizations must be in terms of visual qualities of style, Wölfflin's classic Principles of Art History being a good example. Descriptions must be of elusive visual qualities. I have distinguished sensibility from the traditional concept of imagination where the imagination was the source of rich conceptions of mythological, religious, and historical subjects. The imagination relevant to sensing is the imaginative use of experience with some terms of attention. These brief remarks show how very general linguistic acts and intended perlocutionary forces can be understood within the limits of sensing.

Critics, however, intend perlocutionary forces which are much more individualistic than just these generalized functions. We accept a much broader range of styles in criticism than we do in science or mathematics where there is more agreement on the perlocutionary goals of successful proofs or arguments. Criticism is essentially a literary art, with all the allowance for personal style which that entails. Baudelaire did not intend merely to characterize, describe, and explain with regard to Delacroix and Horace Vernet. Baudelaire even says that the best criticism is poetry,[8] and he sometimes tried to achieve perlocutionary forces typical of poetic arts. He sometimes even uses a line of poetry to describe Delacroix. Baudelaire was also trying to be passionate, partial, and political.[9] He intended to be witty, cutting, and, to Horace Vernet, destructive. We can infer that Fry did not intend these same sort of literary qualities in <u>Transformations</u>. Instead he intended to give clear and detailed analyses of the visual functioning of paintings. Ruskin admittedly is attempting to show us as much about nature as about Turner, and his descriptions of nature, though rather high strung, over-embellished, and distinctly romantic to modern ears, are very different in literary quality from those of Baudelaire. Critics as writers, then, intend to achieve individualistic perlocutionary forces, as well as to satisfy general ends of linguistic acts which have come to be considered a part of a critic's job. This individuality of literary quality extends into the very structure of a critic's writings. Rosenberg tries to do criticism without all the theoretical baggage of Ruskin and Baudelaire, rarely theorizing about what faculty makes great art. The style and structure of modern criticism is radically different from that of the two great nineteenth-century Romantic critics--Baudelaire and Ruskin.

Critic's intentions can be expressed in terms of desired appraisers. Poetic descriptions are intended to achieve appraisers of poetry, and thus positive appraisers ascribe expression of some unarticulated experience to the critic. Descriptions of certain sorts are the more literary-like functions of criticism. Visual explanations, on the other hand, for example, those of Fry in <u>Transformations</u>, are intended to achieve thoroughness, soundness, and a high degree of visual sensitivity. These are more science-like appraisers, and I think it was no historical accident that the new critics and critics like Fry developed at a time when a positivistic spirit was widespread in their culture.[10] Thus certain appraisers come to be loosely fixed to certain linguistic functions. Because of this plurality of quality of linguistic acts, so to speak, it is fruitless to look for a single appraiser which best expresses the sort of convincingness and quality a critic wishes for his various linguistic acts. Margolis' claim that "plausible" is the best appraiser for critical interpretative schemes in his sense of "interpretative" thus seems much more limited in scope than he seems to think.[11] I think it would be rather flat and misleading to characterize Baudelaire's attack on Horace Vernet as plausible, even if we think the attack deserved. A witty and cutting criticism is just not accurately characterized as plausible, though I think one could certainly say some of Fry's detailed and well worked out analyses are plausible. Baudelaire certainly was not trying merely to be plausible.

Margolis might reply to this criticism by saying he meant plausibility to be applied to whole critical points of view, and not to remarks about specific works. But I think this will not do. Critic's writings vary in nature from well worked out theories to loosely organized observations. Baudelaire said he tried to practice criticism without a system of interpretation, being content to express his feeling. Rosenberg has many penetrating observations, but few theories. Ruskin, on the other hand, is full of elaborate theories about everything from truth to the nature of imagination. And thus I think there is no single appraiser appropriate to writings with very different structures, qualities and virtues. Margolis might reply in a second way that plausibility was only a minimal condition so far as perlocutionary force goes, and that a critic's interpretative scheme might have in addition other qualities, such as being witty. "Plausible" then would mean compatible with what is known. This line of argument would be nearer to being correct. But at least for critical verbal functions in certain terms about specific works, I think we claim more than plausibility for interpretative schemes. I emphasize this point shortly in the idea of truth-plus appraisers. I have not attempted to deal, in this work, with the status of critical interpretative schemes with regard to issues such as relativism, though I think I could give a non-relativistic argument for why we accept certain terms of criticism just as I have tried to give and give below non-relativistic arguments for how remarks about specific paintings work.

Perlocutionary Force and the Viewer

Not only are there parameters set, so to speak, on the nature and kind of perlocutionary force desired in various linguistic functions <u>in the culture of the critic,</u> but there are some different parameters (and sometimes different kinds of parameters) set by the <u>viewer's culture</u>. When the readers of a critic are of the same period as the critic, then of course these parameters coincide; but when the readers of a critic are of a later time, some entirely different parameters come to operate. Baudelaire and Ruskin, not to mention Reynolds, seem somewhat quaint to our taste because of the nature and quality of contemporary linguistic functions. Theorizing and a strong commitment to an aesthetic position are now unusual. Modern critics, such as Rosenberg, are much more ad hoc and much less theoretical than traditional critics. Criticism in terms of vague generalities such as beauty, nobility, and the sublime is out. We expect more analytical detail and precision. Our beliefs cause us to prefer certain linguistic functions with certain perlocutionary ends consonant with our culture. These are factors which must be mentioned in any analysis of how critical verbal functions achieve their perlocutionary force.

The viewer's knowledge, beliefs, experience and abilities affect the perlocutionary force intended by a critic on at least two levels--the abstract aesthetic level of arguments for the terms of a critic's criticism and the concrete level of the application of the term to specific paintings. The first level does not really involve sensing as a visual ability. Nevertheless some factors operating at the level of <u>accepting a basic aesthetic position</u> or <u>terms of criticism</u> are these: A critic's <u>arguments</u> or <u>reasons</u> for the terms of his criticism may become convincing. This kind of conviction may come about in many ways. The critic may make criticisms of paradigms one once had valued, and these negative judgments may lie in one's memory and be haunting, despite one's dislike of them. Greenberg's criticism of Kandinsky's failure to understand and develop a modern space was such a remark for me. My estimation of Kandinsky's greatness changed. Since Kandinsky had been a paradigm or model of abstract expressionism for me, his decline meant some basic changes in my aesthetic position. Concomitantly, I was developing a taste for certain other painters which were to become paradigms. This kind of change was growth or evolution at the more abstract aesthetic level, the level of statements about what makes great art, paradigms, defining examples, etc. A change from a traditional expressionism to a purism which emphasized modern plastic space was underway.

There are not-strictly-aesthetic issues which influence perlocutionary force at this abstract level. Art appreciation is really motivated by the moral belief that one should seriously consider what a painter attempted to do. Thus a not-strictly-aesthetic consideration such as fairness influences the sort of linguistic functions and terms one prefers in a critic. At the very least, one must realize that all terms of criticism are not equally fair as applied to some painter. Further, a general objection to the terms of any critic is that those terms have very limited range of application. All these factors are relevant to the perlocutionary force of arguments or reasons for the terms of an aesthetic position.

Sensibility as a visual ability, the second level mentioned above and the only level of perlocutionary force analyzed in this book, is relevant to perlocutionary force when the critic applies the terms of his criticism to specific works. Until a viewer's sensibility reaches at least the stage of sensing as visual exploring, that viewer is in no position to find critical remarks about specific paintings perceptive, sound, etc. As a rank beginner, one is in no position to find Greenberg's characterization of Kandinsky's space sound or Rosenberg's description of Hofmann's "The Bird" perceptive. These appraisers presuppose some experience in sensing Kandinsky and Hofmann. Very often both ability to sense in some terms and experience gained from employing that ability on some group of works is required in order for passages in criticism to achieve desirable perlocutionary forces. What a rank beginner does is ask someone he trusts on aesthetic matters questions such as: Who is a good critic to read on Abstract Expressionism? What sort of position does so and so hold, and is that a reasonable position for a certain kind of painting? etc. The critic's reputation may be important. Also, one might have a taste for the works he discusses. One might find a critic's arguments for the terms of his criticism convincing. There is no question here of finding remarks perceptive or sound or insightful. One does not have any funded experience or ability to sense on the basis of which one can find these remarks about specific paintings sound or perceptive or insightful. A viewer typically will move through stages such as finding remarks completely baffling and not knowing what to make of them, to finding them perceptive or sound, to finding them obvious. Going through these stages is a sign of the dynamics of a developing sensibility.

Since one has <u>to have sensibility</u>, at least of the level of sensing as visual exploring, to find critical remarks about specific paintings sound or perceptive or insightful, viewers at different stages of sensing or the same viewer at different times do not take the critic's verbal acts about specific paintings in the same way. A beginner in learning some terms of attention takes the terms pedagogically, and tries to redistribute his attention in the proper units and kinds of units, as illustrated in my model. A viewer, on the other hand, with considerable experience with that kind of term may immediately find, say, a description insightful or misleading. This difference means there must be some other reasons (besides finding the terms perceptive, etc.) for learning the terms of criticism of some critic, and typical reasons were just mentioned.

One can give a list of perlocutionary forces achieved in the viewer, and, as one might expect, these perlocutionary successes are parallel to intended perlocutionary forces. Poetic descriptions sometimes achieve perlocutionary force expressed in appraisers such as insightful, incisive, perceptive, expressive, articulative of the new, brilliant, sensitive, and penetrating. Successful characterizing wins appraisers such as sound, plausible, reasonable, just, and fair. Explanations and interpretations aim at some of these same more pedestrian appraisers. Successful interpretation takes, in addition, perceptiveness with regard to character. Having a good sense of character to features like physiognomy and posture may be necessary for a great interpretative critic. (See the qualification above in Chapter VI). Comparatives can take the appraisers of erudite art history and the keen eye of the connoisseur. These vary from perceptive and sensitive to sound and plausible. High quality conclusions can be just, fair, deserved, cutting, stinging, damaging, etc. I also reemphasize that these generalized perlocutionary successes have to be supplemented by the more individualistic appraisers the critic was trying to achieve as a writer, as in Baudelaire's obvious intent to be witty. We allow for more individuality of style in critics than we do in science, mathematics, or philosophy.

<u>Truth Plus</u>

When we consider appraisers for expressing how some passage from criticism strikes us, once we have sensibility, we notice the appraisers include more than truth or falsity of the passage. This more or truth-plus may include matters such as expressiveness, appropriateness, highlighting of unnoticed facts, solidifying of things we had sense or felt, etc. Knowledge, including our visual knowledge of paintings, has a structure, and truth-plus appraisers often mean some remarks structured our knowledge. In terms of previously developed concepts, truth-plus appraisers indicate an articulation of our funded experience of some group of works. Put differently, truth-plus appraisers indicate some change on the second cutting edge, the place we are in our particular aesthetic development. "Insightful" and "perceptive" may mean expression of some unarticulated sensing, and they also mean that the quality articulated is significant or important. Remarks we find perceptive or insightful may change the way we view some painter. "Perceptive" often means something we had seen or sensed, but had not attended to, is thrown into relief, and its significance realized. "Reasonable," "just" and "fair," used of characterizations, for example, usually mean that the painter viewed in this way is enriched, and that the terms of viewing do not work against the painter's intention. "Sound," though it means a remark is not exciting, does mean besides true that the remark expresses something well established or something that is really solid and reliable.

Truth-plus appraisers are the kind of appraisers we should expect if developing a sensibility is a dynamic process, for the plus often indicates a remark advanced our sensibility and funded experience in some way such as solidifying it, articulating some funded experience we had not been able to express, pulling together some loose ends, throwing things into better relief, etc. Thus the idea of truth-plus fits well with the concept of a developing sensibility which has stages and styles. Note also that developing a sensibility does not mean the style of that sensibility itself emphasizes originality or rapid assimilation of the new. One may wish and be acquiring a more scholarly type of sensibility, one more like a skill. Even nonaesthetic modes of sensing such as acquiring the eye of a connoisseur, in the sense of a detector of forgeries, have a dynamic development, and truth-plus appraisers are used of them. In summary, the idea of truth-plus covers all stages and styles of sensibility. In many instances truth-plus appraisers are used where no special <u>ability</u> is necessary to see the expressiveness, appropriateness, significance, solidity or fairness of some remark. It was once pointed out to me that Baudelaire refers to more paintings in his first Salon than in all the others put together.[12] This remark is perceptive, for it highlights the increasing tendency of Baudelaire to theorize, but the remark takes no ability to be appreciated. I think, however, that if one returns to the examples from the critics given (Chapter IV), and imagines oneself without experience with the terms of attention used in the examples and without the funded experience of using those terms of attention, one will realize that these remarks cannot be taken as perceptive, insightful, sound, plausible, reasonable, fair, etc., without ability to sense in those terms and/or funded experience in applying that ability to some work or grouping of works.

A legitimate objection to the concept of truth-plus is that appraisers such as perceptive, sound, and insightful should be analyzed as truth-minus. We may use such appraisers when we are too tentative to claim truth. Factors I mentioned as examples of the plus in truth-plus were factors such as expressiveness, highlighting of unnoticed facts, solidifying things we had sensed or felt, etc. As noted, these all have to do with the second cutting edge, the place we are in our particular aesthetic development. Thus they emphasize pedagogy or development more than truth. Shortly, I will give reasons why our awareness of having good judgment in an aesthetic context is less clear than our awareness of having more ordinary forms of good judgment. These reasons have to do with the peculiar nature of painting impressions. Picture space is inviolable and fixed, thus cutting off two main ways we ordinarily know we have good judgment or prognostic perception. Already, it has been emphasized that we have corroboration, but not confirmation of our aesthetic judgments. These are reasons perhaps for saying that concepts like perceptiveness, insightfulness and soundness, when used of judgments of a critic and used to express the perlocutionary force the critic achieves with the viewer, mean truth-minus. The factors noted (expressiveness, highlighting of unnoticed facts, solidifying things we had merely sensed or felt before, etc.) seem to emphasize the pedagogy of developing sensibility more than truth.

My answer is that the idea of truth in the idea of truth-plus is a necessary condition of appraisers like perceptive, insightful, sound, etc. Any critical remark thought to be false could not be perceptive, sound or insightful. The element of correspondence between critical remarks held to be perceptive, insightful or sound and the impression of the painting referred to is essential. The kind of truth involved in critical judgments is "soft" because of the problem of corroboration but not confirmation and because of the peculiarities imposed since picture space is involable and the objects in it are fixed. Thus judgments about objects in picture space are necessarily different from judgments of ordinary prognostic perception. But there is no reason a judgment cannot be held to be true in a tentative way, a judgment that cannot be fully confirmed but can be corroborated. This tentativeness is due to the fact that critical judgments being analyzed here are about impressions of paintings. A crucial idea I have been trying to develop is that the visual sensibility required to evaluate critical judgment is a form of genuine visual judgment even though such sensibility is about a painting's impressions, how the painting really looks, and not about the relation of looks to how the things in picture space really are. Some sense can be given to the question how something really looks, as one of the lines in the Müller-Lyer illusion really looks longer than the other. A theory giving a similar causal explanation of the impressions of a painting is given in the last chapter. The truth in truth-plus appraisers such as perceptive, sound, or insightful is necessarily transformed when that which the critic is expressing is a claim about how a painting really looks, given the special sense being attached to the concept of really looks here.

Some Phenomenological Questions

Earlier I distinguished an act of attention from the noticing which completes the act. Actual visual uptake or noticing, indicated in appraisers such as "perceptive," means some <u>visual</u> facts about some painting or group of paintings now are thrown into relief, now are solidified and organized, now are high-lighted, now are expressed, etc. Truth-plus appraisers at the level of sensing, and ultimately sensing is a visual exploring completed by various kinds of noticing, mean an actual organizing of a painting or group of paintings as a visual field. Fry gets us to organize our attention in terms of plastic qualities and gestalts which include plastic qualities of groups of objects. Ruskin gets us to look at landscapes in terms of meanings to human figures in the paintings and in terms of meanings to the viewers of paintings. All the examples can be treated analogously as involving some actual structuring of the visual field of some painting or group of paintings. The most dramatic illustration of this sort of organizing is visual structuring in a literal sense, as when one first notices or has one's attention drawn to some inter-thing gestalt, such as the triangular structure of Leonardo's "Madonna of the Goldfinch." A crucial question is whether this structuring of paintings as visual facts is imposed or sensed.

There is an active sense in which we __structure__ a visual field and a __receptive__ sense in which we __notice__ the structure a painting already has. No doubt if we take passages from critics as __commands__, specifically directions on how to look at paintings, we can see that they restructure the seeing of those paintings. There is a certain amount of freedom in organizing visual fields. But, if sensing really has a Perceptual Condition and a Subtlety Condition, we do not have freedom to structure the visual field of paintings as we wish. Further, if a painting is a causally active field, as I will argue in Chapter IX, it will already have a structure due to the weighting of variables. Both these conditions (Perceptual and Subtlety) mean the critic articulates what we independently sense. Initially, we can only take passages from critics as commands on how to look at a painting or instructions on how to look at a painting, that is, we can only take the passages pedagogically. But sensing as an ability is a visual exploring completed by various kinds of uptakes. It is these uptakes, provided by the painting itself as a causally active field, which give the passages from critics typical perlocutionary forces such as being perceptive, sound or distorting.

Phenomenologically, if we take passages from critics as commands, some very different things seem to happen visually when different kinds of terms of criticism are involved. See this painting as having a triangular structure (Leonardo's "Madonna of the Goldfinch"); see this painting as imbalanced because of the placement and size of the central figure (Fry on the Daumier); see this painting as having traditional deep space and as not really based on an understanding of the space of synthetic cubism (Greenberg on Kandinsky); see this painting as pavements of light and bituminized bananas (Rosenberg on a Hofmann); and see this painting of Gothic Nudes as having the tone of uprooted bulbs (Clark on Gothic Nudes)--these seem to my eyes to cause very different things to happen to the paintings. I suspect that when we spontaneously find passages from critics to have certain perlocutionary forces such as "perceptive" or "sound," in contrast to seeing paintings on command, there is actually different kinds of visual noticing or uptake involved; but I think the question is an experimental one.

The idea of truth-plus can be related to these speculations and to the earlier distinction between experience with some terms of attention and funded experience. I am uncertain, as just noted, whether very different appraisers such as "sound" versus "perceptive," for example, mean the character of the visual uptake or noticing, in contrast to articulating funded experience, is different. I am more certain that highlighting some fact about a painting or group of paintings or classifying some group of paintings in an interesting and new way or explaining an impression we had merely felt before--any of which involve the idea of truth-plus in appraisers such as "sound" or "perceptive"--indicate an articulation of funded experience or unarticulated sensings. The actual visual uptake, however, may not show such differences as, say, "sound" versus "perceptive" indicate. The eyes do not cut in the same sort of "terms" or "categories" as a natural language, and this difference is the reason it was earlier argued that sensing is a visual act independent of the verbal act from which it was learned. Also appraisers sometimes indicate something about the nature of the whole activity of viewing in contrast to articulation of funded experience alone. To find a critic's characterization of a period of painting sound, for example, means the viewer has carefully studied the works in question. "Sound" is an appraiser which suggests a careful and thorough visual exploring and examining. Thus an appraiser may suggest something about the nature of the visual uptake, articulation of funded experience or the nature of the visual exploring, with emphasis on the latter two.

I do not want to say, however, that we must have already noticed what the critic articulates. Often we have felt something about a composition, say, have felt something was wrong with the composition of the Daumier Fry analyses. But equally often, it is only after a critic has directed our attention to some painting that we notice something not sensed before. But in these latter cases it is presumably our sensing as an ability, sensing as a feeling for the relevant variables for some terms of attention, which is the source of our finding the passage from some critic perceptive, sound, etc. Whether we have sensed a painting as described, characterized, explained or interpreted before or after the description, characterization, explanation or interpretation does not seem to matter. In either case, it is plausible to interpret sensing as an independent visual exploring completed by various kinds of uptakes or noticings. Learning to sense is learning a mode of sophisticated attention, and when that mode is employed on some painting or group of paintings, the object attended to, a painting as a causally active field, provides the convincing. Peirce's idea that nothing is so convincing and inevitable as truth is especially plausible when descriptions, characterizations, interpretations or explanations redistribute attention so that the object itself, in this case the painting, provides an uptake.[13]

Non-Aesthetic Issues and Sensing

One may notice that appraisers often contain meta-critical beliefs, beliefs about what criticism should be. (Sometimes substantial aesthetic positions also may favor certain appraisers, as Romantics emphasize "originality" and related appraisers both for paintings and critics.) Very often these meta-critical beliefs are based on views one has about the nature of originality in painting, and views on how the critic helps us assimilate original works--in other words, beliefs about what I called the first cutting edge. A very different sort of meta-critical consideration concerns what we might call epistemological preference--preference let us say for poetic insight instead of more mundane sureness and certainty. One appraiser (insight) emphasizes a knowledge which has fast turn-over suitable for assimilating the new, and the others (sureness and certainty) a kind of knowledge which is more plodding but more certain. Styles of sensing are very deeply influenced by epistemological preferences. A viewer with epistemological preference for poetic insight would be more attracted to Baudelaire than Fry. A viewer with epistemological preference for more analytical detail, more sureness and certainty with regard to the critic's claims, would prefer Fry to Baudelaire. Epistemological preference has more influence on one's choice of linguistic functions and styles than on one's choice of the terms of a substantial aesthetic position.

A viewer with epistemological preference for poetic insight with regard to criticism need not also have that sort of epistemological preference for more ordinary forms of knowledge. The same viewer might, for most of his ordinary epistemic activities, demand sureness and certainty. He may expect his experience with art to complement or provide relief from his usual mode of knowing. Certainly the phenomenon of a rigorous logician and empiricist combined with a religious mysticism is not unfamiliar in our philosophical tradition. At any rate, a viewer's epistemological preferences for criticism, which amounts to the kind of knowledge he demands from the critic, inclines that viewer to like certain linguistic functions more than others, and epistemological preference is reflected in one's favorite appraisers.

Epistemological preference, and others matter which involve considerations other than sensing, as the consideration of fairness, are more relevant to what I earlier called the style of sensing than to stages of sensing or to sensing in terms of some substantial aesthetic position. One could be developing a sensibility for puristic qualities and prefer the kind of knowledge suggested by "insightful" or the kind of knowledge suggested by the appraiser "sound." And thus what I have said about favored appraisers should connect ideas such as the linguistic acts, critic's intended perlocutionary force and resultant perlocutionary force in the viewer to the model of stages and styles of sensing. In other words, I have tried to show how verbal functions of critics ultimately get assimilated to stages and styles of sensing. We can expect sensing to have the sort of rich plurality of the verbal functions from which the terms of sensing and the style of sensing is learned.

In summary, critic's reasons and conclusions about impressions of paintings, as suggested as early as the Introduction, are rarely connected by formal logic. Rather the critic's reasons may be expressed in any number of linguistic acts, such as describing, interpreting, characterizing or explaining, in certain terms; and conclusions vary from verdicts (Greenberg on Kandinsky) to summary descriptions (Baudelaire's attempt to describe the elusive quality of Delacroix's works). What really bridges the gap in these sorts of "arguments" is some kind of faculty or ability, and on this point I agreed with Sibley. Historically faculties or abilities such as taste or imagination have served this function. I have given a lengthy analysis of sensing as a visual ability or visual sensibility, and I think visual sensibility is the ability presupposed in the arguments of a wide range of contemporary critics--critics as different as naturalists, expressionists and purists. (Now I have shown that perlocutionary force appraisers such as sound, perceptive or insightful mean more than truth, and the truth-plus meant in these appraisers is factors such as expressiveness, appropriateness, highlighting of unnoted facts, solidifying of things we had sensed or felt, characterizing or classing in new and interesting ways, etc.) I have also argued that it is <u>plausible</u> to interpret various kinds of perlocutionary force, which is a <u>linguistic</u> matter, in terms of my theory of <u>visual</u> acts. Specifically I argued that sensing is an ability which includes the concepts of experience with some terms of attention, funded experience and visual uptake in noticing. I especially emphasized that factors such as expressiveness, appropriateness, highlighting of unnoted facts, solidifying of things we had sensed or felt, characterizing or classing in new and interesting ways, etc., have to do with the expression of funded experience accumulated through sensing as an ability. (I suspect there is actual difference in visual uptake parallel to the wide variety of appraisers.) I have unified an abbreviated theory of perlocutionary force of linguistic acts with a theory of visual acts. I have shown that visual acts learned from verbal functions of critics can be independent visual acts of skilled exploring. We judge verbal acts of critics by our visual sensibility, and we express our judgments in various kinds of perlocutionary force appraisers. My theory has epistemological significance because it explains how various kinds of critical reasons about impressions of paintings achieve various kinds of perlocutionary force in relation to critical conclusions. The subject of how critics achieve perlocutionary force, if it does not exhaust the subject of critical reasoning about impressions of particular works, at least explains a good deal of critical reasoning. Of course, I have not dealt, except in passing, with how a critic justifies the basic terms of his criticism. Thus I have dealt with what is called the logic of criticism only at the level of reasons and conclusions about impressions of specific works.

All the various types and levels of perlocutionary force appraisers, of linguistic functions in certain terms, presuppose that the viewer has some funded experience of sensing the painter or paintings. We have to learn to see and sense a painting before that painting can appear in certain ways. My analysis of sensibility is an attempt to characterize the ability to sense. However, having the ability to sense is different from <u>knowing</u> one has the ability to sense, and the latter has important epistemological relevance.

Perlocutionary Force and Self-Knowledge

The most severe problem in terms of self-knowledge that one has sensibilities is that all forms of genuine judgment must be shown in some context. A person who is said to have good judgment about distances must be found repeatedly to be accurate in his visual judgments of distance. A baseball player must have excellent judgment in estimating instantly where a hit ball will land. The possession of good judgment of various sorts (or keen ability to sense in a certain context) is shown in repeated success in the activity. At first there seems no form of activity-testing of sensing. Picture space, for example, is only apparent space, and there is no possibility for comparing the way the space appears to the way it actually is. If it <u>appears</u> to be like the space of late Cubism, it <u>is</u> like the space of late Cubism.[14] If a face appears to be sad, it is sad. In sensing a painting, there is not the usual contrast of the way things are versus the way they appear. Further, unlike in ordinary life, there is not the possibility of waiting to see if judgments about character and emotion have in fact been good judgments. In short, picture space is inviolable and the image is fixed, thus cutting off two main ways judgments about the structure of picture space and the nature of the objects in it could be checked. Any test of whether one really has ability to sense plastic qualities or expressive qualities, for example, seems completely stymied. Thus there is no self-knowledge forthcoming about success in these activities.

Another way of stating this problem is in terms of Aristotle's distinction between special and common sensibles. One meaning of common sensibles in Aristotle is that some qualities, such as shape and mass, have analogues in other senses than, say, vision.[15] Thus there are tactile, and even auditory, analogues of visual shape and mass. Senses other than sight thus can confirm the truth of a visual judgment about the common sensibles in a way that these senses cannot confirm visual judgments about special sensibles such as color. In a painting, however, all qualities, with the exception of surface texture, become special sensibles of vision. Thus shape and mass, for example, have no meaning except how they look. This conversion of common sensibles to special sensibles is another way of stating that if something looks massive in a painting or looks imbalanced in a painting, it is massive or imbalanced.

In summary, picture space is inviolable and fixed, and common sensibles are converted into special sensibles. These factors seem to make it impossible to know one has ability to sense. These factors cast doubt on whether this sort of sensing, in contrast to ordinary prognostic perception, should be characterized as an ability. There are two levels to this problem, self-knowledge of ability to sense in the terms of some substantial aesthetic position and self-knowledge of the nature of sensibility.

Self-Knowledge of Ability to Sense in Certain Terms

It must be admitted immediately that self-knowledge of one's ability to sense in certain terms has a peculiar character when compared to self-knowledge of ordinary forms of prognostic perception, and this peculiarity has already been emphasized. If one has some ordinary ability to sense, such as being a good judge of mass or character, one can have a general awareness of one's ability due to the number of successes and failures one has had. One can also know if a particular judgment one has made is a good judgment. But both one's self-knowledge of a general ability to sense qualities in a painting and awareness of how good a particular judgment about those qualities is have the peculiar character of being entirely determined by dialogue with others. As Tormey put it, we can have corroboration, but not confirmation, of our aesthetic judgments.[16] One can also have corroboration of one's general ability to sense in terms of some aesthetic position. General awareness of an ability just comes from particular successes. But still corroboration by others of how they sense paintings can genuinely demarcate ability to sense from lack of that ability. If, on many occasions, we have sensed various paintings to have plastic qualities, and if a number of these sensings have been confirmed by the descriptions, explanations, or characterizations of others, then we have good grounds for believing we are developing ability to sense this kind of quality. We may often know how something appears to us before that appearance is described, characterized, or explained. Sensing is the ability we develop, involving the direction of visual attention, so that the painting achieves its full range of visual qualities. Suppose one has with regard to many <u>other</u> paintings sensed the <u>sort</u> of quality in question. One has also learned to sense from critics <u>other than</u> the ones in question. Suppose one has been reinforced in this sensing by descriptions, characterizations, etc., of others with regard to this kind of quality. (I emphasize <u>kinds</u> or <u>sorts</u> of qualities because that is the same emphasis <u>I made</u> in discussing the essential generality of terms of attention in Chapter III). Then one gains confidence in his ability to sense this sort of quality.

We can know something about the state of our sensibility along a certain line to what we consider the ideal community of viewers. When we move beyond bare appreciation, paintings begin to <u>appear</u> to have the qualities we could formerly see only on instruction. We actually <u>sense</u> and <u>visually explore</u> in terms of plastic, naturalistic, or expressionistic qualities. Paintings often appear to us to have those sorts of qualities, especially the sort we are learning to sense, and our sensings are confirmed by descriptions of critics and sophisticated viewers in our chosen ideal community of viewers. We can certainly know, at least at times--sometimes paintings do not have a definite and clear look--how a painting looks to us, and when it looks the same way to others in our selected ideal community of viewers, we feel more confident in saying how the painting really looks. Our sensibility is now in the stage of true sensing.

Shortly I collect various objectivistist and anti-relativistic arguments already given on the nature of criticism, and one basic argument can be developed from the points just made. Suppose we have a general awareness of our ability to sense some kind of quality, say the terms of purism. We have achieved this awareness by corroboration from others. Suppose we read a critic on some puristic work and find the criticism perceptive. Since sensing is an ability, and since I shall argue that the painting causes the qualities sensed, our finding the remarks perceptive is not personal and relative. We take the critic's remarks as a perceptive articulation of the paintings analyzed, and I have developed a theory to show that sensing is a visual ability. <u>We cannot check individual judgments the same way we can</u>

<u>individual judgments in ordinary perception, but we can have a general awareness of our ability to sense a kind of quality</u>. In ordinary prognostic perception, for example, having good judgment about distances, we can be aware both of a general ability to judge distances and aware of the correctness of a particular judgment about distance. Still, when we know we have the ability to sense in the terms of purism, for example, we take the critics remarks as articulating the impression of the painting and not as an expression of our own personal visual oddities. A basic part of development of sensibility is our progress from uncertainty and subjectivity in our evaluation of a passage from a critic to assurance that the passage is really perceptive, sound, distorting, etc.

We cannot prove, as already indicated in the remarks on truth-plus appraisers, our ability to sense in the terms of some aesthetic position, as we can prove we have ordinary forms of prognostic perception. We cannot prove that a painting really looks a certain way as we can prove that the way things look are or are not the way they are, as judged by persons with good ordinary judgment of the relevant sort. Still in learning to sense a painting's qualities, we use the same techniques as learning other visual skills. When we have experience with some terms of attention, we accumulate a body of funded experience which needs articulating. Critics articulate this funded experience, showing both their sensibility and our own. This process of self-awareness is more like corroboration than the rigorous process of confirmation in the sciences.

A somewhat different way of putting these points in terms of perlocutionary force appraisers is this: Previously I have said only that the linguistic functions, in certain terms, we find perceptive or insightful or sound are <u>indications</u> or <u>signs</u> of the state and style of our sensibility, but they are not necessarily such indications or signs <u>to us</u>. We often make them become indications to us by asking for some self-reflection from someone we consider a more sophisticated viewer. It is an important and humbling piece of self-knowledge to find that a description we find perceptive is found by others to be obvious. To ask others for their reaction to our appraisers of certain critical remarks is a main way to self-knowledge of the state, style and direction of our sensibility. Of course, such questions show a desire to rationalize our sensibility, in the weaker sense of consciously taking control of its direction, style and state.

One might suspect that there is a sort of vicious circularity here. One sets the direction of his sensibility toward some ideal community of viewers, and that same community of ideal viewers tells one about the state of his sensibility. I have already suggested how I break the circle: Presumably we have learned to sense in certain terms with regard to <u>other</u> paintings and from <u>other</u> critics than the paintings and critic in question. Sensing has this sort of generality. Even though we may have learned to sense in certain manners and terms from an ideal community, seeing and sensing can become autonomous. Not only does the ideal community reflect back to us the state of our sensibility, but also we begin to judge the ideal community in terms of our sensing. Our sensings of paintings or the way paintings appear to us can even force us to change what we consider the ideal community of viewers, though there are always more matters involved in such changes than merely the way paintings appear (for example, all the kinds of non-aesthetic preferences mentioned relevant to aesthetic positions). At first we are excessively dependent on the verbal instructions from our chosen ideal community of viewers, and we are uncertain whether we are sensing or projecting impressions. But later we simply sense certain qualities, and the reader can provide his own examples of such sensings. Somewhat analogously, the beginning astronomer is not certain whether he is seeing the details of a dim galaxy or projecting an image on the sky from some famous description or photograph through a larger telescope. This uncertainty does not mean his seeing can never be autonomous, or that he can never be certain of what he really sees. Some philosophers have exaggerated the dependence of attention on describing (see the quote in Chapter III by White). It seems to me to be true that sensing is not attending under some description; and that we sometimes notice and our visual attention is occupied with subtleties we cannot describe, but later find descriptions for. Thus one argument, already developed, against a general scepticism about ability to sense is the argument for the autonomy of visual acts from verbal acts. A second argument, given shortly, is that sensing a painting as described or characterized can be distinguished from imagining a painting as described or characterized in that only the former is <u>caused</u> by the painting.

Self-Knowledge of the Nature of Sensibility

There is an indirect relevance epistemologically, in terms of self-knowledge, I want to claim for my model. I have claimed that my model and the various ways it can be learned is a systematization of ways we develop various forms of sensibility. If the model is true to the way we learn to sense a painting, it provides some detail on the history of a typical, developing sensibility. This sort of detail, if true, can increase our self-knowledge of the state of our sensibility in the sense of being a general characterization of what sensibility is. The first, and most directly relevant, form of self-knowledge, epistemologically speaking, is our awareness of the stage of our sensibility as a substantial aesthetic position. The latter is our awareness of our ability to deal with a certain kind of term, awareness of our experience in sensing in certain terms, which is a different matter from an awareness of what sensibility in some more general sense is. But my characterization of sensibility is relevant to this more general kind of self-knowledge in the sense of clarifying the nature of the activity of sensing. Knowing what sensibility is and what stage we are in are two different levels of self-knowledge.

Relativism

Since my discussion of perlocutionary force of critical verbal acts is in effect a study in the rhetoric of criticism, the usual relativistic flavor of a study of rhetoric may be left. Further, the special problems of self-knowledge of ability to sense with regard to paintings leaves lingering tones of relativism.

A non-relativistic argument involving the ideas of perlocutionary force is this: Rationality or objectivity may be understood, in the context of criticism of painting, as giving more weight to epistemological appraisers, such as "perceptive" or "incisive," than to a substantial aesthetic position. Let us take an example. We may prefer, let us say, expressionism. But epistemologically we prefer a tight fit for linguistic functions; that is, we want the terms of our aesthetic position to be perceptive, incisive, and penetrating. We may begin to feel that expressionistic terms cannot deliver these qualities. We do not so much feel they are false, as a bit off key everywhere, which is a sign of wanting a new conceptual map. When I read Reynolds, as much as I appreciate him, I feel as though the concepts of nobility and the sublime are not so much false as out of style. Further, sometimes even against our will, some direction-guiding remarks on painters we had previously liked begin to haunt us. An unfavorable verdict on a paradigm of expressiveness may begin to exert its influence. We may gradually <u>come to believe</u> or <u>grow to believe</u> the unfavorable judgment. Concomitant with the terms coming to seem unable to deliver the punch we desire of a close fit in verbal functions, we may be moving to a new aesthetic position. Not only may a negative judgment on some paradigm come to haunt us, but also <u>arguments</u> for some other aesthetic position, usually arguments which take a definite stance on the art-life relation, may become convincing. Of course an argument for the terms of some critic is not evaluated by sensibility except in the sense that the terms may not deliver, to a developed sensibility, the kind of knowledge one wishes from a critic. <u>Ability to sense</u> is relevant to the terms of criticism not at the level of argument, but at the level of application of those terms to specific paintings. In summary our epistemological preferences may ultimately change our substantial aesthetic position, because the terms of the criticism cannot deliver what we desire of verbal functions. There is sometimes this much rationality in basic aesthetic decisions. Any reader who has gone through some growth in the development of his sensibility can find examples like this hypothetical one in his own experience.

The example above is one in which epistemological preferences override a preference for a substantial aesthetic position, and that is another way of saying we may <u>rationally</u> or <u>objectively</u> come to give up one aesthetic position and choose another.

Another non-relativistic and rational way of thinking of a critic's basic terms is that, hopefully, there exists a redundancy between the high level theorizing of a critic and his terms, in linguistic functions, about specific paintings. In a sense the principles and arguments, which are simply the high level theoretical commitments and claims in a critic, are redundant with the experience of viewing <u>if</u> the principles and arguments actually articulate <u>the experience</u> that the specific linguistic functions, in certain terms, formulate. When the verbal arguments and principles of a critic at least accurately articulate the ideal experience of viewing for that critic, there is a sort of redundant congruence between the critic's theorizing and the actual experience of viewing in his terms. Giving a good argument is one kind of objectivity. Sensing as a mode of perception is another. These two forms of objectivity may reinforce each other. This congruence gives confirming support for both the terms of the critic and the arguments justifying those terms. If the theoretical arguments and principles do not truly express the experience of viewing as indicated in the verbal functions about specific paintings, the abstract part of a critic's theory and the actual experience of viewing do not have the same center of gravity. This divergence is another way of saying the critic may have mis-described, mis-characterized, mis-explained, etc., with respect to his models. Then there is the wider question, even if the high level theorizing is accurate to his models and defining examples, of whether that experience in a form of life fills the need which the critic's arguments have said to constitute the aesthetic.

I do, below, introduce a kind of relativism, but it is not the usual relativism with regard to criticism. Let us look ahead: Sensing is affected by matters such as the nature of the eye, scanning habits learned in activities such as reading, basic knowledge of how to distinguish solids, liquids and gases by their looks, knowledge of artifacts, etc. These all affect the impression the Müller-Lyer illusion gives us. Some of these factors are affected by cultures. Impressions of paintings are caused by cues, and basic cues to fundamental qualities such as mass and distance may be different in very different natural-cultural environments. Cultures which have almost entirely rounded artifacts, such as buildings, perhaps are not affected by the Müller-Lyer illusion in the say way we are.[17] Different cultures expose different textures of different kinds of objects and substances, to take an example. These textures of kinds of objects and substances are materials for sensing. In the same manner, different cultures may sense paintings in different ways, though there are no doubt some significant overlaps due to the universality of vision. But notice that this sort of relativism is due to differences in normal vision in a culture. Applied to sensing, this conditioning means that there is some relativism with regard to sensing, but the relativism is due to differences in visual normalcy (the Selective Knowledge Condition) as exploited by the painter. It is not that criticism is especially relative, but that paintings as causally active fields work differently for differently conditioned forms of vision.

Presumably impressions of paintings will be explained in the same way as the Müller-Lyer illusion, and when the impressions are so explained we will have causal explanations of why certain critics' interpretations, descriptions, explanations and characterizations of certain paintings worked and others did not. Since I think that the explanation of impressions of both paintings as causally active fields and the Müller-Lyer illusion is a <u>causal</u> explanation, my theory of sensing does not introduce a relativism about criticism. The ultimate reason certain descriptions, interpretations, explanations and characterizations survive and others do not is that only certain passages of criticism are adequate to the paintings they are about when paintings are functioning as causally active fields. Since the terms of purism, expressionism and naturalism have survived for a long time, they are suitable for paintings which work as causally active fields to eyes conditioned in roughly the way western cultures condition vision. There are some, seemingly large number of, paintings for which each of these aesthetic positions gives suitable terms of viewing. And the concept of styles of sensing, in contrast to the terms of sensing, does not introduce considerations which are relativistic. One viewer might prefer a synoptic and fast moving critic who is interested in assimilating the new. Another might prefer a more analytical and careful approach. I see no reason to doubt that there are paintings, understood as causally active fields, for which these different styles of viewing are most suitable. The same painting, in fact, might have synoptic subtleties and subtleties of detail. The idea of <u>styles</u> of viewing was introduced in the belief that some considerations other than sensing are involved in desired appraisers and that these considerations allow a freedom of choice which does not distort a particular painting as a causally active field.

Impressions of paintings and other sorts of visual impressions have at least these contributing factors: 1) The physiology of the eye (complementary colors). 2) Deep-seated habits such as scanning habits (probably relevant to right left and vertical horizontal asymmetries of paintings). 3) Basic knowledge of artifacts and natural objects in a culture (seeing corners of buildings in "rectangular cultures" may be a partial explanation of the Müller-Lyer illusion). These are all causal matters. The impressions of paintings certainly include these three, for we know all three kinds of cues have been exploited by painters. A painting impression, however, unlike those of illusion illustrations, is a delicate impression which can easily be warped by the terms of viewing. Certain terms of viewing, once one is skilled in them, allow the painting to realize its impression. The correct terms of viewing for a painting are those which allow the painting to realize its full range of impressions. Classical aesthetic positions, such as purism, expressionism and naturalism, are simply terms of viewing which fit the impressions of large numbers of paintings. They allow the painting to <u>cause</u> its impression. No relativism is called for here. Given the nature of the eye, given habits such as scanning habits, given basic knowledge of the relation of looks of things to their wider properties, and given the physical variables having to do with light, there just are approaches, techniques and devices which will allow one to see and sense things which other approaches, devices and techniques would obscure or make invisible. The interaction of these factors can be enhanced or hindered.[18] Various aesthetic positions are simply trial and error discoveries of "natural" terms of viewing.

A persistent skeptic might ask how we know we are looking at a painting and sensing it in certain terms instead of looking at it and imagining it as described, characterized, etc. My reply is this: A general distinction can be drawn between something visually appearing a certain way and something being imagined a certain way. Wittgenstein cited examples showing the contrast between seeing something a certain way and imagining something a certain way. A triangle can be imagined to be hanging from its highest apex or to have fallen over, but it does not truly appear in these ways. Yet a drawing of a cube appears as a cube, and we do not simply imagine it that way.[19] We do not just imagine one of the lines to be longer than the other in the Müller-Lyer illusion. <u>Sensing</u> as I have analyzed it, with the emphasis on cues exciting a background of visual normalcy thus causing the painting to give a wide range of impressions, <u>is in the same family as sensing visual appearances and impressions</u>. I mean for my analogies between sensing a painting's qualities and sensing a longer line in the Müller-Lyer illusion to be taken seriously. The causal field model, explained in the next chapter, gives a theoretical way of distinguishing sensing from imagining as. Sensing has been defined as a subtle kind of perception. Thus sensing a painting, if the painting is understood as a causally active field, means the painting must actually cause the impression sensed. This distinction between sensing and imagining does not mean, however, that we have any grounds for believing our manner and terms of looking at a _particular_ painting are ultimate; and thus we cannot say with assurance that a certain particular description, characterization, explanation, etc., of an impression is perceptive or not without qualification. An answer to general scepticism does not mean we can know with any certainty that we sense a particular painting or group of paintings a certain way in contrast to imagining them that way. I am not suggesting that by some sort of careful visual phenomenology we can tell whether we are sensing or imagining some painting or group of paintings to appear as characterized, described, explained or interpreted by a critic. "Sensing" is a success verb, but we may be uncertain whether some specific critical passage involves sensing or imagining the painting or group of paintings as described, characterized, interpreted or explained. Thus even though I think I succeed, especially given Chapter IX, in delineating sensing from imagining as, and thus answer general scepticism, I have not answered, and doubt one can answer, scepticism about some particular example from criticism on some specific work or works.

    An earlier argument also can be reintroduced to answer the skeptic. I can give a general characterization of the difference between sensing and imagining as, though this general characterization does not settle any specific disputes about sensing. In general, "sensing" has been defined to mean that a painting gives a certain impression because of cues exciting a background of visual normalcy. In the case of imagining, the subject simply projects something on the painting. To use Wittgenstein's example, there are no cues causing us to imagine a triangle as hanging from its apex as there are cues causing a drawing of a cube to appear three dimensional. Imaginings have no basis in visual normalcy, that is, they do not involve the exploitation of the painting as a causally active field. Sensing as a perceptual mode requires that I can distinguish sensing from projecting in that the former involves genuine impressions achieved by exploiting cues from normal vision. It might also be noted that esoteric sensings, as caused by peculiarities of ingrained individual takings, are not the same as imaginings. Since there are individual differences in our backgrounds of visual normalcy, a painting may genuinely give me an impression it does not give you.

In summary, these criticisms of relativism and scepticism can be pulled together by collecting the objectivist arguments I have given, including, in the last one, an argument developed fully in the last chapter. 1) Whenever epistemological preference for some linguistic quality, such as perceptiveness or incisiveness, forces a change in a substantial aesthetic position, then this change is an instance of objectively or rationally giving up an aesthetic position. 2) A critic's argument for his aesthetic may be reinforced by sensing in the terms of his criticism. The objectivity of argument may be reinforced by the objectivity of sensing as a perceptual mode. 3) We can have self-knowledge of our ability to sense in certain terms. This general awareness of ability to sense in certain terms does not mean we can be certain of any particular judgments. But this general awareness, learned from others after we have developed a kind of sensibility, is the basis of progressing from uncertain and subjective reaction to critics' remarks to finding those remarks really perceptive, sound, distorting, etc. 4) If visual acts really are independent of verbal acts, we can visually explore and accumulate a body of funded experience or unarticulated sensings which is material for critical expression. The articulation of unarticulated sensings is a plausible way of thinking of what an appraiser such as "perceptive" means. 5) Sensing means something found out by some subtle mode of perception, that is, it includes the Perceptual and Subtlety Conditions. It may be that sensings are relatively rare, and I have not speculated on the extent of sensings, though I do think instances of sensing are very common. If sensing does mean some mode of subtle perception, then the object sensed must be objectively present as sensed. 6) I have explained universal sensings as being due to cues present in many cultures, such as cues to distance and mass. The nature of the eyes, scanning habits and universal experiences of interacting with objects are the source of cross-cultural impressions. Culture bound sensings are due to artifacts and natural environments peculiar to cultures, such as rectangular and square buildings. Cues can be even more esoteric and personal. At any rate, an explanation of universally sensed impressions, such as space or masses of objects, is an explanation of the objectivity of those qualities. Critical claims that are universally or very widely accepted simply borrow their objectivity from the universality of the impression they are about. 7) Finally, when my analysis more intimately connects, in the next chapter, perlocutionary force with the concept of paintings as causally active fields, the objectivist character of my theory of sensing will be complete.

ENDNOTES

[1] J. L. Austin, *How to Do Things with Words* (Oxford: Clarendon Press, 1963), pp. 101-103.

[2] In characterizing various linguistic functions of critics, I have tried to be sensitive to the ordinary sense of the labels I use, but I am more certain that the content of the analysis is what critics actually do in writing and speaking than I am of the ordinary sense of my labels.

[3] See for example, his long interpretation of "The Return of the Prodigal Son." Diderot, *Oeuvres Esthétiques*, selected by Paul Vernière (Paris: Editions Garnier Frères, No date given), pp. 549-50.

[4] Baudelaire, p. 106.

[5] *Ibid.*, p. 141.

[6] Ruskin, V, 296.

[7] Baudelaire, p. 65.

[8] Charles Baudelaire, *The Painter of Modern Life and Other Essays*, Trans. and ed. by Jonathan Mayne (London: Phaedon Press, 1964), p. 125.

[9] Baudelaire, *Art in Paris*, p. 44.

[10] Christine McCorkel, "Sense and Sensibility: An Epistemological Approach to the Philosophy of Art History," *The Journal of Aesthetics and Art Criticism*, 34 (Fall, 1975), p. 40.

[11] Joseph Margolis, "The Logic of Interpretation," in Margolis, ed., *Philosophy Looks at the Arts*, pp. 108-118.

[12] Professor Joseph Sloane, in a lecture on Nineteenth Century French Art, at the University of North Carolina in Chapel Hill in 1967.

[13] Charles Sanders Peirce, *Collected Papers of Charles Sanders Peirce*, ed. Charles Hartshorne and Paul Weiss (Cambridge, Mass.: The Belknap Press of Harvard University Press, 1974), V, sec. 50. (5.50 in the usual Peirce notation.)

[14] Kivy thinks there is and must be a distinction between appearance and reality with regard to a quality such as the unity of a musical work. A work can appear unified and not really be unified (pp. 5-9). For reasons which will appear shortly, I shall make a more qualified claim about painting qualities such as balance or unification. Most of the qualities discussed by critics of painting are qualities of illusionistic phenomena such as picture space, volumes in picture space, dynamic qualities of objects in picture space, etc. These illusionistic qualities are caused by the painting, and the way in which they are caused will be discussed in the last chapter. Kivy discusses the Müller-Lyer illusion, an illusion which continues to work even when we know about the illusion (pp. 12-14). Painting illusionistic qualities have the same status, and thus even though a painting really appears spatial, volumetric, dynamic, etc., we know it is not really so, and I think we need a different distinction than the contrast of appears versus reality. Awareness that qualities such as balance and unity are qualities of illusionistic qualities should make us cautious about claims about real volumes in a painting or real dynamic qualities in a painting. I will argue that we should instead contrast really appears, meaning how the painting works causally given the nature of the eye, with various forms of imagining or projecting into the painting image. Thus I think my distinction between really appears, for example, spatial versus being imagined to be spatial is not as different from Kivy's distinction between reality and appearance as it first looks! My analysis is definitely not relativistic, and thus some such distinction as Kivy draws needs to be made. But I will argue that with regard to most painting qualities the distinction needs to be drawn in a different way.

[15] Aristotle, De Anima, 418 a 5-19.

[16] Tormey, pp. 35-49.

[17] Gregory, p. 161.

[18] I think one could develop a theory of natural kinds for terms of viewing of paintings, though it would be a theory of natural kinds Aristotle would perhaps not recognize (because of emphasizing learned things such as scanning habits and knowledge of artifacts and natural objects in a culture).

[19] Wittgenstein, p. 193.

CHAPTER IX

SENSING, ICONS AND NATURAL SIGNS

The Selective Knowledge Condition requires, it may be recalled, that certain kinds of knowledge are excluded from sensing. The Perceptual Condition also means that sensing is a perceptual act and not a cognitive act (such as inference). One does not sense the meaning of a sign like the cross nor the meaning of an event like Caesar's crossing the Rubicon. The Selective Knowledge Condition became important in the history of painting with the decline of traditional religious, historical and mythological subject matter and with the impact in Europe of works from foreign cultures, such as Negro sculpture, about which the viewer knew nothing. Fry, in a passage already quoted, gives a good formulation of the Selective Knowledge Condition in his explanation of the emotional elements of design:

> Now it will be noticed that nearly all these emotional elements of design are connected with the essential conditions of our physical existence: rhythm appeals to all the sensations which accompany muscular activity; mass to all the infinite adaptations to the force of gravity which we are forced to make; the spatial judgment is equally profound and universal in its application to life; our feeling about inclined planes is connected with our necessary judgments about the conformation of the earth itself; light again, is so necessary a condition of our existence that we become intensely sensitive to changes in its intensity. . . . It will be seen, then, that the graphic arts arouse emotions in us by playing upon what one may call the overtones of some of our primary physical needs.[1]

There were several arguments for the Selective Knowledge Condition. One was an anti-iconographic (in Panofsky's sense) and anti-historical tradition which emphasized new values in painting such as the importance of still lives and landscapes. These reasons were perhaps sound in the disputes over the direction of painting at a certain time, but are not sound as contemporary arguments, and I have emphasized that sensing as defined here is in no way meant to be anti-iconographic. Panofsky repeatedly uses his sensibility to show that the nature of subject matter as sensed is compatible with and mutually supportive of whatever iconographic interpretation he is giving. A second, more useful, argument is that sensing is a mode of perception. If one claims to have sensed something, one claims to have found it out by some kind of subtle perception, and not by knowledge of symbols or historical events. A third argument that has been mentioned in passing is that sensing is a part of common sense, and common sense does not require a knowledge of iconographic symbols or knowledge of historical and mythological events. This tradition has some of the anti-iconic and anti-historical overtones of the first argument, and I emphasize only the second line of argument.

An artificial division of sensing into its aspects will be helpful in analyzing how paintings cause impressions: We can contrast the passive and causal setting up of a painting world with the active employment of a developed sensibility on the painting world so set up. This distinction is artifical because the impressions a painting causes determine how the painting world and its objects will be judged, and sensing as perceptual judgment likewise enters the determination of the cause of a painting world. These aspects will be temporarily separated by analysis of the causal concepts of cues and animation as compared to the active judgment concept of weighted variables.

Cues and Animations Causing a Painting World: Paintings As Causally Active Fields

The way the painter makes a painting which is a causally active field creating impressions is by exploiting cues and animation from <u>ordinary perception</u>. An ordinary cue to space, texture for example, can be used so a painting will give a sense of space. The concepts of cues and animation need an explanation.

<u>Cues</u>

I use the concept "cues" inclusively, to cover diverse ways impressions of paintings are caused. These vary from strictly physiological causes to indirect effects which presuppose types of experience and knowledge. Taken literally, "cues," as the very concept suggests, presupposes basic experience, and thus cues include more than matters of eye physiology. We normally say texture is a cue to distance and mass, and thus the most literal meaning of "cue" is experienced correlations, such as overlap of objects as a cue to spatial structure. Complementary colors are not really cues to more intense color. I think the reason it is odd to speak of them as cues to more intense color is that we believe complementary colors work because of the physiology of the eye. Also, one of the complementary colors does not seem a sign of the other. That complementary colors intensify each other does not seem like a sign learned from experience. Thus "cues" as here used covers not only appearances caused by cues in the sense of experienced correlations, but appearances caused by the physiology of the eye. Finally, sometimes a concept with more part-whole, instead of causal, connotations is needed. In Leonardo's "Madonna of the Goldfinch," the three main figures are grouped in a pyramid shape. We might call this shape an inter-thing gestalt. The separate figures, however, are not cues to a triangular shape. They are more parts of a triangular gestalt, but I think it is natural to say they give the impression of being a triangular group. This last sort of impression is, of course, quite commonly exploited by painters in spatial composition. Thus I am using "cues" to cover strictly physiological causes, cues and part whole-relations, all of which must work, given the Selective Knowledge Condition, because of the nature of the eye and because of basic experience in which our physiological mechanisms are conditioned.[2]

    The cues exploited by painters need not be universal across cultures, though it seems reasonable to think that overlap and change of overlap with motion are universal cues to distance. But cultural activities such as making things, for example, cause considerable change in natural objects. These changes are shown in both implements or tools and in artifacts resulting from the use of tools. In a common sense way, activities of making things expose parts of objects, such as the inside of trees, and thus increase the range of visual textures relevant to visual judgments. Some activities of making artifacts recast substances so that they come out in an entirely different form, as molten metal and melted glass, and these artifacts further increase the range of materials for visual judgments. Subjects in a hypothetical culture learn correlations, uncovered in making artifacts, between the looks of these objects and other qualities. Subjects in a culture which has metal, glass and plastic will be able to make some visual judgments about other qualities of these objects, such as mass, that subjects in cultures lacking these objects will not be able to make. A painter in a culture which has made metal, glass and plastic can exploit cues entirely lacking in other cultures. Thus since artifacts expose and conceal the correlations of visual cues with other qualities, paintings might have some qualities which work in some cultures but not in others. There is some evidence, in fact, that the Müller-Lyer illusion does not work as well in cultures which have rounded artifacts, such as houses, as in cultures with square and rectangular structures.[3] Analogous arguments can be given about subcultures and about peculiarities of an individual's environment. To take an individual as an example: There may be some peculiarities an individual has repeatedly found to be a cue to some quality important to him. If that cue is present in a painting, the individual will have an impression of the quality the cue is usually a cue to. In sum, the cues painters exploit vary from universal ones to culture bound ones to merely personal cues.

Cues differ in their origin as well as in their universality. In fact their origin is related to their universality or lack of it. A cue which works because of the very nature of the eye, as complementary colors or overlap, is completely universal. Experience of basic categories of things such as solids, liquids and gasses is extremely universal, and visual cues of these objects work across cultures. Learned scanning habits, such as those in reading, are much less widespread, and it is suspected that such differences affect, for example, asymmetries of left and right in picture space. The texture of a very peculiar object found in one culture provides a background of normalcy that only a painter in that culture could exploit.

I emphasize that cues do not have to be consciously articulated. One may sense that one of the lines in the Müller-Lyer illusion is longer than the other without being able to say what cue is causing this sensing. One may give this general explanation of the Müller-Lyer illusion and of other forms of impressions: Some deep-seated knowledge, dispositions of the eye, ingrained visual habits, the nature of the eye, etc., are excited in some way to cause illusions and impressions. The visual cues must be potentially specifiable, but not necessarily specifiable given present knowledge. The qualities we sense in paintings can be given the same general explanation we give for the Müller-Lyer illusion. Painters have known since the renaissance, for example, that texture, overlap, aerial perspective and size constancy affect picture space. Thus the cues in paintings are in theory specifiable in just the same way that cues causing other illusions, such as the Müller-Lyer, are in theory specifiable. Visual cues as causes work when looked at even if we cannot articulate those causes.

Animation

The concept of cues is a causal concept, and thus a cue is always a cue to something like depth or volume. Many idioms we use in speaking of paintings are causal. We say a painting gives an effect of deep space. Cubistic paintings often cause an impression of a shallow and stage-like space. We speak of objects in paintings giving the effect of being instable, etc. But there is an important phenomenon which is not causal, except in the indirect sense that it tends to cause us to judge or take things in picture space to have certain qualities, namely similarities between objects in the painting and ordinary objects.[4] These similarities cause the painting image, in an extended sense of "cause," to be animated by the tones and qualities of ordinary objects or materials or substances or aspects of some object. Animation means that the parts of the painting image are visually formed by tones and qualities of ordinary and odd objects. Here the idiom is less causal because animation works when our visual "vocabulary" comes to enliven and determine the things in picture space. Similarities are not really cues. In fact, expressions of similarities, such as Clark's metaphor comparing Gothic Nudes to uprooted bulbs, appear much more in descriptions and characterizations, while cues are cited in explanations. We must examine animations which work because of similarities in the painting image to ordinary things, aspects of things, materials, etc.

The concept of animation is best explained by recalling some elementary facts about how paintings are made. A "thing" in a painting is never put together the way its represented real thing is. Factors which influence the nature of the things in picture space are:

Paintings are frequently made by preliminary grounds, washes over these grounds and over other washes, drawing which shows all the influences of the painter's training, etc. Almost all, and sometimes all, the elements of art influence the way the final painting and the things in its picture space look. Since this is a typical way paintings and things in picture space are constructed, the painting object never is exactly similar to its represented object.

The similarities to ordinary things exploited in animation may be limited or extensive. It is as though we have a full "vocabulary" of visual images of ordinary objects, places, relations, substances, materials, odd things like clouds, cross species qualities such as being vegetable or animate, etc., and the painter can cause the painting image to be animated by this vocabulary to the degree and in the manner he desires. Brush stroke and other means of painting can be used to create all kinds of similarities to ordinary objects and odd things. Drawing can vary from a realistic projection to a mere suggestion or hint of things, as one can see suggestions or hints of horses in some of Kandinsky's abstract naturalism.[5] Paint texture, by which I mean the texture of the paint on the actual surface of the canvas, can remind us of things, as a drop of red reminds us of blood. This sort of texture is eliminated in realistic works, often with elaborate layers of varnishing. A painter can call as much or as little attention as he wishes to the fact that a painting is painted, by emphasizing or de-emphasizing paint texture. Visual texture, which is texture one can see but not feel, has enormous possibilities for tapping qualities of things and odd things. There are wide ranges of atmospheres and light both in realistic works and abstract works. A painter may use a full range of elements of art, say outlining, textures of objects, light, and atmospheres on the objects, etc., to imitate a full range of aspects of things, and then we have realism; or a painter may have only hints or clues or suggestions of objects, where only a few of the elements of art pick up resonances with things, as in De Kooning's "Woman" series there are pieces, hints, and suggestions of women (the "slipping glimpses," as Rosenberg expresses it).[6] The painter can set up many or few resemblances to ordinary and odd things. The kinds of resemblance and the kinds of objects resembled are very rich and varied. Paintings vary from highly realistic ones in which all the subactivities of painting are used to give a realistic representation to those which, while still representational, allow the elements of painting to follow their own inertia to those abstract works which indulge in the distinctness of elements of art, and thus have very tenuous relations to any ordinary things. Holbein's "Erasmus of Rotterdam" does not just suggest a man, but Rosenberg claims certain Pollocks and Hofmanns give a sense of place.[7] The process of setting up these resonances with ordinary and odd things is what I call "animation."

One should note that not only does animation work to give things in picture space, even picture spaces of abstract paintings, ordinary qualities and tones, but animation can work to make the "things" in picture space distinctively painting things. Our ordinary knowledge includes knowledge of substances which can be smeared and can leave traces of the implements of application. This sort of knowledge of substances and materials has an obvious relevance to animating heavily applied oil pigment. This kind of animation works to make the painting "things" distinctively painting things. Of course, the painter can emphasize the quality of the paint itself as much or little as he wishes. But we do need to note that our ordinary knowledge of things, substances, materials, aspects of things, etc., not only animates the painting things with qualities of things in the world, but may animate the painting things with qualities peculiar to the nature of the medium and to the method of application. Thus purists need not object to all styles of animation.

I have deliberately included in my exemplifying list of kinds of things which can animate paintings (ordinary types of objects, aspects of these objects, materials, substances, places, relations, odd things such as clouds, cross species qualities such as being vegetable or animate, etc.) a very rich list from the point of view of categories. Any number of kinds of things or kinds of ways of considering them make up the vocabulary which animates the painting image. Specifying animation is so difficult and verbally demanding because of the category richness of things which may animate the painting image. Earlier I spoke of category flux and crossings (such as planes of color or shapes of holes) as being characteristics of paintings. Given the way things in a painting are made, such richness is inevitable. Expressing category richness requires verbal and other forms of creativity on the part of the critic (for example invention of some new reference aiders). Category flux and crossing is largely caused by animation.[8] Original painting thus requires the critic to use creative reference aiders, metaphors, and even intermediate aids to help the viewer see in terms appropriate to the original work.

The <u>nature</u> of the things in picture space is largely determined by the visual "vocabulary" of ordinary objects which animate the painting image. A long analysis would be required to explain fully how we grasp the nature of things in visual judgment, but here only a sketch can be given. By "the nature of things" I mean the total set of characteristics of just this object in just this place. If we identify the species of some object, we know the <u>range</u> of the nature of things of that kind. Tigers are the sort of animals to be ferocious. But type identification has been excluded from the definition of aesthetic sensing since the Subtlety Condition is not satisfied by ordinary identifications. One does not sense a man in Holbein's "Erasmus of Rotterdam." And if a figure is somehow hidden in a painting and one has to do some detective work to find it, then this is a kind of sensing which is not aesthetic.[9] But we employ a wide range of visual abilities on features and aspects of things <u>other</u> than those relevant to <u>species</u> identifications. We have a vast visual knowledge of substances, materials, textures, orientations of objects, kingdoms of plants and animals, etc., as contrasted to species limited knowledge. The painter can exploit any of this cross-species or trans-species knowledge by similarities which cause the painting thing to be animated by the qualities desired. The full range of these animations determine the nature of the particular thing in this particular picture space. Visually judging the nature of some thing then goes considerably beyond identifying the species of the thing, and it requires attention to the sort of cross-species aspects and features suggested (materials, substances, orientations, kingdoms, etc.).

Visually judging a thing's nature, of course, does not exclude species identifications. Without species identifications one would often misjudge the nature of the thing, as one knows at least a range of qualities about the nature of an animal when he identifies the animal as a tiger. But judgment about the nature of this particular thing in this particular picture space goes beyond type identification. And judgments about the nature of a thing does pass the Subtlety Condition of sensing. One does not sense a man in Holbein's "Erasmus of Rotterdam," but one does sense qualities of the man represented. In sensing the particular nature Erasmus is represented as having in this particular painting, one employs some of our vast visual knowledge of things other than knowledge of features relevant to mere species identification. There are obviously deep and complex metaphysical-epistemological issues here which need sorting out to have a complete theory of how we perceptually judge a thing's nature, and I have here only attempted some sketchy clues. (I have some dim intuitions about how to develop a metaphysical realism to show how the nature of the eye, by visual acts, can be better fitted to the nature of the thing seen.)

I have repeatedly said sensing is a success word, and if we sense something a certain way it must be that way. Thus sensing a thing's nature, in ordinary perception at least, must be supported by other knowledge about that thing's nature. Sensing is only the **perceptual** way of grasping a thing's nature. I did note an important oddity of visually sensing with regard to picture space—one can check one's judgment about the nature of something in picture space only by dialogue with others.

Animation is most conspicuous in works which are naturalistic or expressionistic. The painter can hardly purport to give insight into nature unless there are at least hints of things in the work. Further, we naturally speak of very powerful works, such as Picasso's "Guernica," as being suggestive. It is animated by images of human and animal terror. But I do not confine animation to naturalistic or expressionistic works. Plastic qualities are also affected by animation. There is a very great difference between a space with fluffy, cloud-like forms in it and one with lead-like and massive forms in it. Thus the nature of objects in picture space, of puristic, expressionistic or naturalistic works, is determined to a large extent by the objects which animate the image. Also of course whatever cues the work exploits determine the nature of the picture space and the qualities of objects in the picture space. Thus, animation and more-strictly-causal effects work at the same time and are not visually presented in a separate way. A brush gesture that suggests something is almost bound to determine something about the picture space.

The concept of paintings as causally active fields

can now be defined in terms of the concepts of cues and animation. All "causally active field" here means is the sum total of causal dispositions a painting has because of cues and animations of the painting image. By "causally active" I mean some visual mechanism, either innate or very basically conditioned, can be excited to create an impression of space. Thus, "causally active" means that something one sees, perhaps something one cannot specify, causes the painting to appear some way, as seeing something in the Müller-Lyer illusion, a visual cue or cues not at present specifiable with certainty, causes one of the lines to appear longer than the other. A closed figure, for example, will set up a figure ground relationship creating a sense of space. Complementary colors intensify each other for some causal reason which is not now clear. Textures, atmospheres and overlaps will create a sense of space. Animation determines the nature of the objects in picture space. The concepts of cues and animation complete my analysis of the idea of paintings as causally active fields.

In summary, both cues and animations determine the structure and nature of picture space and determine the nature of the objects in picture space. Also in summary, the explanation of how paintings work, through cues and animations, passes the Selective Knowledge Condition in the definition of sensing. Ordinary motor knowledge, such as that texture is a sign of space, is the source of cues and animations which set up the painting world through the painting as a causally active field. The background of visual normalcy, in other words expected correlations between qualities such as texture and space or solidity, exploited by painters requires no knowledge of iconographic traditions nor knowledge of the meaning of particular historical events or personages. Thus sensing of impressions caused by paintings as causally active fields is a genuine perceptual act.

If my analysis of paintings as causally active fields is correct, Goodman's comparison of painting to a kind of language is fundamentally mistaken.[10] In my view, paintings do not have a syntax or semantics, but work by using cues which excite, both in cues and animations, our ingrained expectancies. I agree with Wollheim that if representation is a code or a language based on convention: "We have not a picture that we look at, but a puzzle that we unravel."[11]

A Speculative Explanation of Cues and Animation

Empirically, in terms of theory of vision, the explanation of how the range of cues and animations in paintings as causally active fields work is of course a long way off. Even the Müller-Lyer illusion cannot be explained with any certainty. But I can give a philosophical model, consistent with the above remarks about visual judgments, of paintings as causally active fields.

A way of discussing correlates which set up painting worlds or correlates which make a painting a causally active field is to use Chisholm's concept of "taking," one of the conditions of perceiving. Taking is an especially suitable concept for my theory of sensibility because it covers both verbally articulated judgments and motor judgments. Since takings can be non-verbal judgments, takings can be related to the claim that sensing, as in the case of the painter, for example, can be learned from nonverbal activities. Further, a theory of takings which explains what constitutes a background of visual normalcy shows takings can satisfy the Selective Knowledge Condition. If the only knowledge required of a viewer is knowledge acquired in takings in motor activities, that viewer can pass the Selective Knowledge Condition. "Taking" means more than being appeared to, presumably some sort of judgment is involved. Judgment can be shown linguistically or behaviorally. Taking, as Chisholm understands it, is judgment about objects, their characteristics, and anticipated causal interactions with these objects.[12]

Chisholm develops the idea of causal interaction with objects in terms of changes of our position with regard to the object. In other words, if we now take an object in a certain way, and if we move, we anticipate future takings; and if these come about as anticipated, our original taking is confirmed. For example, if we judge that a near object will loom up as we approach it, and if it does loom, we confirm our original taking that it was close. Chisholm's concept of causal interaction can be enriched. Surely we should include actual changes we make in the objects, and not just changes made in the way objects appear as we move. And surely we can include causal changes objects themselves make, as in their development. In other words, a present visual taking is relevant to future takings as the result of three kinds of causal interactions with objects: Changes in the way objects appear, changes we actually make in objects and changes which objects themselves undergo.

The idea of taking can be expanded to include basic expectancies. Suppose that in interacting causally with an object, an original visual taking has been consistently followed by other takings, visual and otherwise. When we have judged an object, on the basis of a taking on its visual texture, to be solid, we move towards it, and we have visual takings of looming and eventually tactile takings of resistance and expulsion. We will come to expect that the visual texture, as judged, will be followed by an orderly series of takings, visual and otherwise, when the same sequence is followed.

It is easy to give other examples of visual takings in relation to other expected qualities of things. We have visual ability to distinguish solids, liquids and gasses. We have ability to judge from a thing's visual textures and form gesture what sort of mass it is likely to have. We learn that the look of stone means a massive object. Further, things have typical gestures of shape or outline. By "gesture of outline" I mean that a material such as glass does not have the same gesture as pewter; and visually we not only key on the texture of glass versus a pewter pitcher, for example, but also on the gesture of outline. A further extension still of visual knowledge of things is the orientation of objects, orientation being crucial in visually detecting dynamic qualities of things, whether things are about to collapse on us, whether things are stable, whether they are so stable, because of mass and orientation, as to make moving them possible or impossible, etc. Further, we know how to tell visually whether things are inanimate, vegetable or animate. These categories all have different characteristic textures and gestures, though of course there are confusing cases. Matters such as those just discussed are correlations relevant to perceiving a thing's nature.

It is obvious that an infant, at a fairly young age, develops a very rich knowledge of how visual takings, say of texture, will be related to future takings, visual and otherwise, when certain things are done to or in relation to certain objects. As an adult, our visual takings are confirmed by other takings, both visual and otherwise, in the vast majority of cases, and we are very surprised when our basic takings, based on present visual judgments, are not followed by expected takings. It is this body of expected correlations between the present visual taking and future takings, visual and otherwise, which the painter exploits. In fact, these basic expectancies are simply the cues already emphasized.

Cues and animations, such as the exploitation of texture so as to create a sense of space, presuppose only a background of visual normalcy in a viewer. Thus it is clear that impressions of paintings can be achieved given the Selective Knowledge Condition. The correlations between visual takings and other takings are set up in ordinary motor experience. No special knowledge of symbolism or knowledge of particular events in history or mythology is necessary for the painting as a causally active field to work. Further, it might be noted that the explanation of effects I have given in terms of takings and basic expectancies is very similar to Fry's explanation, at the beginning of this chapter, of the emotional elements of design.

Sensibility as Judgment Employed on Causally Active Fields

In the introduction to this chapter, I proposed, for purposes of analysis, isolating the passive and causal setting up of a painting world from the active employment of a sophisticated visual judgment, a developed visual sensibility, on this painting world. Now some summary remarks are necessary to show that the development of sensibility in some aesthetic terms of attention (for example, purism, expressionism or naturalism) passes the Selective Knowledge Condition. More importantly, I must summarily pull together previous strands of argument to show that sensibility to paintings is a genuine form of visual judgment. It is certainly true that having ordinary visual _motor_ knowledge is not the same as having the ability to sense in terms of some aesthetic position. I emphasized that ordinary sensibilities, such as to distance or character traits, do not have a direct carry-over to painting contexts. The way sensing as a seated ability was analyzed was: One learns to discount and emphasize visually in the manner suitable for some terms of attention. The model of a visual act is an idealization of how we learn visually to attend to a painting. With practice one develops experience with those terms of attention. The developed ability to sense, which is the same as experience with some terms of attention, can vary in nature from visual skills to responsive noticing. It was also especially emphasized that one must employ visual attention on the critic's models and defining examples, for it is in these paintings that we can most literally see what the critic means by some term like "significant form." Certainly paintings having the status of models and defining examples are not ordinary objects perceived and handled in motor activities. Nevertheless, the way I analyzed developing a set of weighted variables through experience with paintings in certain terms of attention was distinctively a method for developing visual ability, and not a method for learning the meaning of symbols or learning the meaning of language. The model of a visual act emphasizes learning to see and sense in the literal sense of employing the eyes, assisted by aids and techniques such as pointing and gesturing, on visual objects. The introduction of models and defining examples does not change this emphasis. Sensing of models and defining examples is quite literally sensing their visual impressions. And the weighting of variables developed in experience with painting is analogous to the development of other visual abilities such as having good spatial judgment or having good judgment about character (the latter, of course, always includes more than visual ability).

When the Selective Knowledge Condition was introduced, it was emphasized that this condition is not just negative and exclusive but also positive. Even though a viewer may not be expected to have knowledge of religious, historical and mythological symbols, much more is expected of the viewer's visual experience and knowledge. He is expected to have experience with some terms of attention, to have exercised that ability and to have accumulated some funded experience of visual traditions and styles of painting. This new expectation of wide visual experience is a byproduct of the museum phenomena, of the easy availability of prints, of easy travel and of the development in art history of the concept of visual style. Thus even though less is expected of a viewer in one way, more is expected in another. The Selective Knowledge Condition places high requirements on the knowledge (visual) selected. Also, of course, there is no reason a highly developed visual sensibility has to exclude knowledge of iconographic traditions, though this knowledge is not a matter of visual sensibility.

Finally, this summary shows that sensing as an

ability, the kind of visual judgment employed on the realized painting impression, does pass the Selective Knowledge Condition. I have tried to explain both the setting up of a painting world and the employment of visual judgment on the realized impressions in terms of visual experience, both ordinary experience and experience with paintings as models and defining examples. Ordinary motor experience generates the correlation of cues with expected qualities which the painter exploits to cause impressions. And the development of experience with some terms of attention is a matter of discounting, emphasizing and focusing attention appropriately on models, defining examples and other paintings.

Natural Signs

The concept of cues understood as basic correlations between qualities such as texture and space and the concept of animation, that is the theory of a painting as a causally active field, are easily connected to a wider philosophical theory, namely the theory of natural signs. In fact, the way I have analyzed the setting up of a painting world and the nature of visual judgment employed on it entails a theory of natural signs, so one must be briefly defended.

Thomas Reid nicely states the distinction between artificial and natural signs, but his grounds for the distinction are not adequate. Signs are of two kinds: "First, such as have no meaning, but what is affixed to them by compact or agreement among those who use them; these are artificial signs: Secondly, such as, previous to all compact or agreement, have a meaning which every man understands by the principles of his nature."[13] And again, when things "are connected by the course of nature, it is a natural sign; when by human appointment, it is an artificial sign."[14] "Thus, smoke is a natural sign of fire; certain features are natural signs of anger; our own words, whether expressed by articulate sounds or by writing, are artificial signs of our thoughts and purposes."[15] Natural expressions of thought include modulations of the voice, gestures, and features.[16] And Reid explicitly connects natural signs to the arts: "It were easy to show, that the fine arts of the musician, the painter, the actor, and orator, so far as they are expressive; although the knowledge of them requires in us a delicate taste, a nice judgment, and much study and practice; yet they are nothing else but the language of nature, which we brought into the world with us, but have unlearned by disuse, and so find the greatest difficulty in recovering it."[17] Reid's emphasis on natural signs as being things "connected by the course of nature" will be expanded below, but his argument that artificial signs are based on compact or agreement while natural signs are not will not be emphasized, though there is no indication in the text that Reid believed artificial languages originated by any actual compact or agreement.

Alston seems to think signs can be distinguished from symbols on the basis of the regular correlation or fixed spatio-temporal relation of the sign to its object, and this is perhaps a way Reid's distinction between natural and artificial signs can be made.[18] Some of Alston's examples are causal, as in "a rapid pulse is a sign of fever," but others involve mere correlation, as "pottery fragments are a sign of human habitation." Symbols, on the other hand, are constituted by the fact that there exists a regular practice of use of a sign for something as in "that whistle means that the train is about to start" or "'thermometer' denotes an instrument for measuring temperature." I think regular correlation is not a strong enough relation to distinguish signs from symbols and situations of use when a symbol is well established. I think we should push the distinction in the direction Reid suggests in his phrase "course of nature," and I have already indicated in analyzing Chisholm that I think the key idea is that natural signs have some causal relation to their object. Chisholm, it will be recalled, made causation a part of the meaning of taking. If we visually take an object a certain way, we expect the appearance of that object to change in orderly ways as we move in relation to the object. I suggested that two further causal relations be included in taking--changes we actually make in the subject, in contrast to changes in its appearances due to movement only, and changes the object undergoes of its own nature and disposition. Causality, enriched to include these three senses, I think is an adequate basis for distinguishing natural signs from symbols. Knowledge of natural signs, then, is that body of knowledge we accumulate, in causal interactions with objects, of causal relations between signs and objects. Such causal knowledge is independent of knowledge of symbols. Animals give every indication of having a knowledge of natural signs in the sense of knowledge of causal correlations between signs and objects or events. And thus this way of analyzing natural signs satisfies the Selective Knowledge Condition.

One might reply in criticism of the distinction between signs and symbols on causal grounds that with a sufficiently advanced physiological and psychological theory one could give a causal explanation of the connection of symbols to their objects, a connection via patterns of conditioned behavior, etc. Two comments seem in order here: In the first place, no such causal laws are forthcoming, nor even any in sight. Second, and more importantly, even if such laws were forthcoming, the laws presumably would not require the connection <u>of just that symbol</u> with its object. There are laws of phonetics, but these laws only set outside parameters on sounds used by cultures, and the laws no doubt contain the truth that certain physiological organs, conditioned by long habit, will not be used to make just any sounds for words. But the connection of natural signs to their object is much more than this; <u>the sign itself</u> has a causal connection to its object, and Reid perhaps had an intimation of this relation in his suggestion about connection by the course of nature. Rising thermometers do not have the same sort of relation to fever as the sound for "man" or the written symbol "man" has to men. Some other sound or written sign could be substituted, given parameters of English phonetics, with no infringements of laws of nature. Thus natural signs are expressions of causal laws.

It is also important to notice that natural signs are emphasized by naturalists and expressionists, and <u>perhaps</u> are not exploited at all by purists. As just intimated, natural signs <u>mean</u> their object, as a high thermometer means fever or black clouds mean rain or blood means suffering and possible death. Any painter, or critic interpreting a painter, who wants to give insight into nature or wanted to exploit expressive power will exploit the meaning of natural signs. We also need to notice that painters are interested only in <u>certain</u> natural signs. Most natural signs do not have much dramatic significance or possibility so far as insight into nature goes. Only dramatic natural signs or signs which possibly can give insight into nature will be of interest to an expressionistic or naturalistic painter. Crudely speaking, painters are interested in those dramatic natural signs which have some fairly direct connection with the meaning of life, and natural signs of this sort can be exploited even if one wants to assert that life has no meaning. I am uncertain whether to say purists exploit natural signs or not, but I think this uncertainty does not matter. It does seem normal to say texture and overlap are signs of space, but less natural to say they mean space, and there may be something to the purist dictum that certain paintings do not mean but are. Also, it seems true that purists do more to exploit certain impressions of painting than to exploit animation and suggestiveness of painting. But it is certainly true that naturalists and expressionists exploit elements of art which mean something, and the basis of this exploitation of ordinary vision I have claimed is natural signs based on causal correlations learned in ordinary motor activities.

A necessary condition of sensing defined with a Selective Knowledge Condition is a distinction between natural signs and symbols, for the Selective Knowledge Condition excluded the meaning of symbols or knowledge of particular historical, religious and mythological events. I have tried to show that there are natural signs, and that Reid was right in distinguishing what he called natural signs from artificial signs. If we cause something, in a genuine perceptual sense, the something must be a natural sign.

ENDNOTES

¹Fry, <u>Vision and Design</u>, pp. 34-35.

²Like Reid, I do not think we can distinguish at the phenomenological level what is physiological from what is learned in basic experience, for the two extremes, nature and nurture, are inextricably interwoven before we could be interested in self analysis. See Thomas Reid, <u>An Inquiry into the Human Mind, on the Principles of Common Sense</u> (Glasgow: W. Falconer, 1819), p. 130.

³R. L. Gregory, <u>Eye and Brain: The Psychology of Seeing</u> (New York and Toronto: McGraw-Hill, 1966), p. 161.

⁴Like Peirce, I think the distinction between icons and symbols is a real distinction. Icons, but not symbols, are similar to the object represented. (<u>Collected Papers</u>, 2.276) It is certainly true, as Goodman observes, that in terms of <u>total</u> number of similarities any two cows are more similar to each other than a painting is to any cow, but I think Goodman is informing no one in this perhaps humorous remark, because the defenders of the distinction between icons and symbols have never meant more than <u>limited</u> similarity. The limited similarity between a picture of a cow and a cow is easy to state, and Leonardo's advice to young painters, to practice drawing on a pane of glass, shows the two similarities I want to defend. If one traces the outline of a cow on a pane of glass, the visual angles and proportions cut by the cow in our visual field will be the same as those visual angles and proportions cut by the painting as viewed from a single point of view, the point of view where the painter's eye was located as he traced the outline. If this is not a real similarity I do not know what is. Astronomers, surveyors, etc., are continuously measuring visual angles, and objects which cut the same visual angle are similar in this respect. If cows have different shapes and are positioned so that difference can be seen, and if the shape of one of them be traced on a pane of glass, that shape on the pane of glass will be more similar in the limited respect of visual proportions to that cow than the other cow is to that cow in this limited respect.

I do not know of anyone who has ever thought that, in terms of total similarities, a picture of a cow was more similar to that cow in all respects than that cow was to any other cow.

A second real similarity is color. Suppose the young painter in Leonardo's example was instructed to exactly match the colors on the pane of glass to the original. (This would of course give other similarities as well, such as aerial perspective or chiaroscuro.) The painting on the pane of glass would now have two real similarities to the cow, and actual paintings have these same two similarities to their subject matters (the same visual angle, given a certain point of view on the subject and on the painting, and the same colors). Of course, different kinds of paintings have more or less of these two similarities. Highly realistic works are those in which the painter has focused all the elements of painting, such as drawing, light, chiaroscuro, color schemes, etc., so that the similarities will be as close as possible. Yet abstract paintings may have only hints or suggestions of objects, as in the figments or fragments of horses discernable in Kandinsky's work as he made the transition to abstract paintings. Many modern painters use only figments or fragments of subject matter in their work, as Rosenberg well states in referring to the slipping glimpses of objects in de Kooning's works.

[5] An active way of speaking of a painting, instead of saying it is animated by ordinary objects, is to say the painting suggests some object. I will use "animation" and "suggestion" as meaning the same except for causal direction. "Animation" means a painting is caused to have qualities of ordinary objects. "Suggestion" means a painting gives some allusion to objects. In de Kooning's Woman series, one can say the painting is animated by figments, parts and fragments of women. One can also say these figments, parts and fragments suggest women.

[6] Rosenberg, <u>The Anxious Object</u>, p. 96.

[7] <u>Ibid</u>., p. 69.

[8] Since painting images are constructed and thus are pervaded with pulls and stresses of the act of painting, even the most realistic images are metaphoric in showing the thing represented in some new categories and manners.

[9] One does, if Rosenberg is right, sense landscapes in certain Hofmanns and Pollocks. But Rosenberg does not mean we find some hidden gestalt in them.

[10] Goodman. The whole book develops his argument, and thus no particular pages can be cited.

[11] Richard Wollheim, "On Drawing an Object," in Joseph Margolis, ed., <u>Philosophy Looks at the Arts: Contemporary Readings in Aesthetics</u>, Revised edition, p. 266. Originally given as a lecture at the University of London.

[12] Chisholm, <u>Perceiving</u>, pp. 79-86.

[13] Reid, pp. 90-91.

[14] <u>Ibid</u>., p. 323.

[15] <u>Ibid</u>.

[16] <u>Ibid</u>., p. 92.

[17] <u>Ibid</u>., p. 94.

[18] William P. Alston, "Sign and Symbol," <u>The Encyclopaedia of Philosophy</u>, ed. Paul Edwards (New York: Macmillan Publishing, 1972), VII, 439-40.

BIBLIOGRAPHY

Alston, William P. "Sign and Symbol," The Encyclopedia of Philosophy, ed. Paul Edwards. New York: Macmillan Publishing, 1972.

Anscombe, G. E. M. Intention. Oxford: B. Blackwell, 1963.

Aristotle, De Anima.

Aschenbrenner, Karl. The Concepts of Criticism. Dordrecth and Boston: Reidel, 1974.

Austin, J. L. How to Do Things with Words. Oxford: Clarendon Press, 1963.

Austin, J. L. Philosophical Papers, ed. J. O. Urmson and G. J. Warnock. Oxford: The Clarendon Press, 1962.

Baudelaire, Charles. Art in Paris, 1845-1862: Salons and Other Exhibitions, trans. and ed. by Jonathan Mayne. London: Phaidon Press, 1965.

Baudelaire, Charles. The Painter of Modern Life and Other Essays, trans. and ed. by Jonathan Mayne. London: Phaedon Press, 1964.

Beardsley, Monroe C. Aesthetics: Problems in the Philosophy of Criticism. New York, Chicago, San Francisco, Atlanta: Harcourt, Brace and World, 1958.

Bell, Clive. Art. New York: Capricorn Books, 1958.

Chisholm, Roderick M. Perceiving: A Philosophical Study. Ithaca, New York: Cornell University Press, 1957.

Chisholm, Roderick M. Theory of Knowledge. 2nd ed. Englewood Cliffs, N. J.: Prentice-Hall, 1977.

Clark, Kenneth. The Nude: A Study in Ideal Form. Garden City, N. Y.: Doubleday Anchor, 1956.

Dickie, George. *Art and the Aesthetic: An Institutional Analysis.* Ithaca and London: Cornell University Press, 1974.

Diderot. *Oeuvres Esthétiques,* selected by Paul Vernière. Paris: Editions Garnier Fréres, n.d.

Dretske, Fred J. *Seeing and Knowing.* Chicago: The University of Chicago Press, 1969.

Fry, Roger. *Transformations: Critical and Speculative Essays on Art.* London: Chatto and Windus, 1960.

Fry, Roger. *Vision and Design.* New York: Meridian Books, 1960.

Gibson, James J. *The Senses Considered as Perceptual Systems.* London: 1968.

Gombrich, E. H. *The Story of Art.* London: Phaidon, 1966.

Goodman, Nelson. *Languages of Art: An Approach to a Theory of Symbols.* Indianapolis and New York: Bobbs-Merrill, 1968.

Greenberg, Clement. *Art and Culture: Critical Essays.* Boston: Beacon Press, 1967.

Gregory, R. L. *Eye and Brain: The Psychology of Seeing.* New York and Toronto: McGraw-Hill, 1966.

Gregory, R. L. and E. H. Gombrich, eds. *Illusion in Nature and Art.* New York: Charles Scribner's Sons, 1973.

Grice, H. P. "Meaning," *The Philosophical Review,* 66 No. 3 (1957).

Hardie, W. F. R. "The Final Good in Aristotle's Ethics," *Philosophy,* 40 (1965).

Hester, Marcus. "Purpose in Painting and Action," *American Philosophical Quarterly,* 7, No. 1 (January, 1970).

Hume, David. *A Treatise of Human Nature,* ed. L. A. Selby-Bigge. Oxford: The Clarendon Press, 1958.

Husserl, Edmund. *Ideas: General Introduction to Pure Phenomenology*, trans. W. R. Boyce Gibson. London: George Allen and Unwin, 1958.

Isenberg, Arnold. "Critical Communication," *The Philosophical Review*, 68 (July, 1949).

James, William. *The Will to Believe and Other Essays in Popular Philosophy*. New York: Longmans, Green and Co., 1897. Reprinted in Amelie Rorty, ed., *Pragmatic Philosophy: An Anthology*. Garden City, N. Y.: Anchor Books, 1966.

Kandinsky, Wassily. *Concerning the Spiritual in Art, and Painting in Particular*, trans. Michael Sadleir, Francis Golffing, Michael Harrison and Ferdinand Ostertag. New York: George Wittenborn, 1966.

Kivy, Peter. *Speaking of Art*. The Hague: Martinus Nijhoff, 1973.

Margolis, Joseph, ed. *Philosophy Looks at the Arts: Contemporary Readings in Aesthetics*, revised ed. Philadelphia: Temple University Press, 1978.

Margolis, Joseph. "The Logic of Interpretation," *Philosophy Looks at the Arts; Contemporary Readings in Aesthetics*, revised ed. Philadelphia: Temple University Press, 1978.

McCorkel, Christine. "Sense and Sensibility: An Epistemological Approach to the Philosophy of Art History," *The Journal of Aesthetics and Art Criticism*, 34 (Fall, 1975).

Neisser, Ulric. *Cognition and Reality: Principles and Implications of Cognitive Psychology*. San Francisco: W. H. Freeman and Company, 1976.

Panofsky, Erwin. *Studies in Iconology: Humanistic Themes in the Art of the Renaissance*. New York, Evanston, and London: Harper Torchbooks, 1962.

Peirce, Charles Sanders. *Collected Papers of Charles Sanders Peirce*, ed. Charles Hartshorne and Paul Weiss. Cambridge, Mass.: The Belknap Press of Harvard University Press, 1974.

Poggioli, Renato. *The Theory of the Avant-Garde*, trans. Gerald Fitzgerald. New York, Evanston, San Francisco, London: Harper and Row, 1971.

Reid, Thomas. *An Inquiry into the Human Mind on the Principles of Common Sense*. Glasgow: W. Falconer, 1819.

Reid, Thomas. *Essays on the Intellectual Powers*. Cambridge, Mass., and London: MIT Press, 1969.

Reynolds, Sir Joshua. *Discourses on Art*, ed. Robert R. Wark. San Marino, Calif.: Huntington Library, 1959.

Rorty, Amelie, ed. *Pragmatic Philosophy: An Anthology*. Garden City, N. Y.: Anchor Books, 1966.

Rosenberg, Harold. *The Anxious Object: Art Today and Its Audience*. New York and Toronto: Mentor, 1969.

Rosenberg, Harold. *The Tradition of the New*. New York and Toronto: McGraw-Hill, 1965.

Ruskin, John. *Modern Painters*. London: George Allen, 1903.

Schwyzer, H. R. G. "Sibley's 'Aesthetic Concepts'," *The Philosophical Review*, 72 (January, 1963).

Shaffler, I., ed. *Philosophy and Education*. Boston: Allyn and Bacon, 1958.

Sibley, Frank. "Aesthetic Concepts," *The Philosophical Review*, 68 (October, 1959).

Tormey, Alan. "Critical Judgments," *Theoria*, 39 (1973).

Vesey, Godfrey. *Perception*. Garden City, N. Y.: Anchor Books, 1971.

White, Allan R. *Attention*. Oxford: B. Blackwell, 1964.

Wittgenstein, Ludwig. *Philosophical Investigations*, trans. G. E. M. Anscombe. New York: Macmillan, 1960.

Wollheim, Richard. "On Drawing an Object," in Joseph Margolis, ed., *Philosophy Looks at the Arts: Contemporary Readings in Aesthetics*. Revised edition. Philadelphia: Temple University Press, 1978.

Ziff, Paul. "Reasons in Art Criticism," in Margolis, ed., *Philosophy Looks at the Arts*. New York: Charles Scribner's Sons, 1962.

INDEX

Alston, W. P., 154,159.
Anscombe, G.E.M., 41,52.
Aristotle, 50,79,123,137.
Aschenbrenner, K., 94.
Austin, J.L., 21,31,39,100,103,136.
Baudelaire, C., 1,2,5,6,14,15,16,17,18,19,21,22,24,25,
    35,56,64,65,68,69,70,72,76,78,95,96,99,103,106,
    107,108,110,111,112,114,116,121,136.
Beardsley, M. C., 8,24.
Bell, C., 5,12,25,35,99.
Cezanne, 33,43,50,53,58,61,76,95,96,107,109.
Chisholm, R.M., 28,38,52,149,154,159.
Clark, K., 63,70,72,83,84,86,94,107,118,143.
Daumier, 1,32,58,59,63,66,70,118,119.
Delacroix, 14,18,19,68,69,70,76,86,87,95,96,99,107,
    108,110,121.
Dickie, G.,24.
Diderot, 36,106.
Dretske, F.J., 7,12.
Fry, R., 1,5,15,16,17,19,20,22,24,25,32,35,39,57,63,64,
    66,70,72,86,87,95,96,97,103,106,110,111,117,119,
    120,157.
Gibson, J.J., 1,37,52.
Gombrich, E.H., 9,12,22,69,70,72,92.
Goodman, N., 58,72,148,157,158.
Greenberg, C., 1,67,70,72,96,99,112,113,118,121.
Gregory, R.L., 9,137,157.
Gregory, R.L., & E. H. Gombrich., 26.
Grice, H. P., 52.
Guston, P. 18,68.

Hardie, W.F.R., 94
Hester, M., 26.

167

Hofmann, Hans, 18,58,62,68,71,83,100,113,118,145,159.
Holbein, Hans, 31,33,38,145,146,147.
Hume, D., 16,21,24,25.
Husserl, E., 52.
Isenberg, A., 45,52,83,85.
James, W., 22,26.
Kandinsky, W., 25,67,112,113,118,121,158.
Kivy, P., 9,12,137.
Margolis, J., 8,12,94,111,136.
McCorkel, C., 136.
Moore, G.E., 25.
Neisser, U., 100,103.
Panofsky, E., 5,12,35,139,140.
Peirce, C.S., 36,100,120,136,157.
Picasso, 67,70,96,99,147.
Poggioli, R., 65,72.
Pollock, J., 18,47,67,68,70,96,99,100,107,145,159.
Reid, T., 36,44,52,153,154,155,157,159.
Reynolds, Sir J., 1,5,13,17,18,19,22,24,35,112.
Rorty, A., 26
Rosenberg, H., 1,5,17,18,20,22,24,25,68,71,73,83,94,
    95,100,103,110,111,112,113,118,145,158,159.
Ruskin, J., 1,2,5,6,15,16,17,18,19,22,24,35,58,63,64,
    65,67,72,95,96,100,103,106,108,110,111,112,117,
    136.
Schwyzer, H.R.G., 7,12.
Shaffler, I., 39.
Sibley, F., 1,7,8,9,10,12,30,38,121.
Tormey, A., 94,124,137.
Turner, J., 58,60,63,67,68,95,96,100,108,110.
Vesey, G., 38.
White, A., 43,52,127.
Wittgenstein, L., 44,45,52,53,56,64,65,72,76,78,132,
    133.
Wollheim, R., 109,159.
Ziff, P., 31,39,84,94.

DATE DUE

SEP 2 '86

DISCARDED BY
DARTMOUTH COLLEGE LIBRARY